AUDEN AND DOCUMENTARY
IN THE 1930s

Marsha Bryant

AUDEN AND DOCUMENTARY
IN THE 1930s

University Press of Virginia

Charlottesville and London

Acknowledgments for previously published material appear on page xii

The University Press of Virginia
© 1997 by the Rector and Visitors of the University of Virginia
All rights reserved
Printed in the United States of America

First published 1997

⊚ The paper used in this publication meets the minimum
requirements of the American National Standard for Information
Sciences—Permanence of Paper for Printed Library Materials,
ANSI Z39.48–1984.

Library of Congress Cataloging-in-Publication Data

Bryant, Marsha, 1960–
     Auden and documentary in the 1930s / Marsha Bryant.
          p.   cm.
     Includes bibliographical references (p.   ) and index.
     ISBN 0-8139-1756-5 (alk. paper)
     1. Auden, W. H. (Wystan Hugh), 1907–1973—Knowledge—Motion
pictures. 2. Motion pictures and literature—Great Britain—
History—20th century. 3. Literature and society—Great Britain—
History—20th century. 4. Documentary films—Production and
direction—Great Britain. 5. Documentary films—Great Britain—
History and criticism. I. Title.
PR6001.U4Z625   1997
811'.52—dc21   97-19689
                                                                                    CIP

for Sybil, Tweed, and Camden

CONTENTS

ILLUSTRATIONS

ACKNOWLEDGMENTS

MY INTEREST in W. H. Auden began with B. J. Leggett's course in modern British poetry, which I took as an undergraduate at the University of Tennessee. I would like to thank him for a stimulating introduction to the sheer variety of Auden's work. Since that time, a number of other people have shaped the course of this book. I am grateful to Cary Nelson, my dissertation director at the University of Illinois, for his astute comments on the early stages of my research. Because he elicited rather than imposed ideas, this project has continued to be intellectually exciting for me. Some of my work on this book was supported by Research Development Awards from the University of Florida. Several colleagues have been generous with their comments on my revisions: R. B. Kershner, Patricia B. Craddock, Alistair Duckworth, Caryl Flinn, and Malini Johar Schueller. Two journal editors, Evelyn J. Hinz (*Mosaic*) and Morton P. Levitt (*Journal of Modern Literature*), provided valuable feedback on earlier versions of chapters 2 and 3, respectively. I thank Edward Mendelson for writing *Early Auden* and for granting me permission to reproduce Auden's photographs. Stephen A. Smith helped me locate President Clinton's citation of "In Memory of W. B. Yeats." My colleague Elizabeth Langland gave me good advice about selecting a publisher. And thanks to Cathie Brettschneider, my editor at Virginia, I have found publishing an academic book to be a humane and even pleasurable undertaking.

I am grateful to my parents, Sybil and Tweed Bryant, and especially my husband, Camden Pierce, for tolerating this book's intrusions on family life. Finally, I give thanks for my son, Nicholas, whose recent arrival has given a sense of balance to our household.

EXCERPTS FROM *The English Auden: Essays and Dramatic Writings 1927–1939, The Dyer's Hand and Other Essays,* and *Selected Poems* are reprinted by permission of Faber and Faber. Excerpts from *Letters from Iceland, Journey to a War,* and *Plays, and Other Dramatic Writings by W. H. Auden, 1928–1938* are reprinted by permission of Curtis Brown and of Faber and Faber.

Portions of four poems from *W. H. Auden: Collected Poems,* by W. H. Auden. edited by Edward Mendelson, are reprinted by permission of Random House, Inc.: "In Memory of W. B. Yeats," copyright © 1940 and renewed 1968 by W. H. Auden; "The Watershed," copyright ©1976 by Edward Mendelson, William Meredith, and Monroe K. Spears, Executors of the Estate of W. H. Auden; "I Am Not a Camera," copyright © 1972 by W. H. Auden; "September 1, 1939," copyright © 1940 by W. H. Auden.

Portions of chapter 2 appeared in "Auden and the Homoerotics of the 1930s Documentary," *Mosaic* 30, no. 2 (June 1997): 69–92. Most of chapter 3 appeared in *Journal of Modern Literature* 17, no. 4 (1991): 537–65, as "Auden and the 'Arctic Stare': Documentary as Public Collage in *Letters from Iceland.*"

AUDEN AND DOCUMENTARY
IN THE 1930s

1

INTRODUCTION

The Auden Generation Meets
the Documentary Decade

IN A 1996 essay for the *New Yorker,* Nicholas Jenkins points out that W. H. Auden's status has reached its highest point in over half a century. Moreover, he notes that Auden's reputation "has carried him beyond the confines of the merely 'literary' audience." The English-born writer who often struggled over his social role has indeed crossed over from the classroom anthology to a broader domain. A featured performance of Auden's poem "Funeral Blues" in the 1993 film *Four Weddings and a Funeral* has increased public awareness of his love poetry. More recently, President Clinton's 1995 invocation of "In Memory of W. B. Yeats" in the wake of the Oklahoma City bombing has continued public uses of Auden's words to address catastrophic human suffering.[1] It is no coincidence that both poems are products of the 1930s.

Best known as a poet, Auden established his literary reputation in a decade framed by economic depression and global war. His frequent allusions to Marx and Freud, along with his uncanny ability to charge words with a sense of impending crisis, gave the young writer an unmatched currency during this time of social instability. Quickly emerging as the voice of his generation, Auden would become a controversial figure in literary and academic circles. Because his thirties writing often adopted leftist stances on such issues as labor unrest and the rise of fascism, Auden's career has served as a litmus test for critics who debate the relationship between art and politics. The greatest controversy surrounding Auden—his emigration to America in 1939—has also accrued political overtones. Some have interpreted this move from war-torn Europe as Auden's move away from social concerns in his writing, while others have argued that he continued to address them, albeit in a different style. Although the degree of the American Auden's progressivism remains debatable, the fact that his later poems often interrogate the dominant culture is not. For example, "The Shield of Achilles" (1952) shows how a violent society blurs boundaries between "A crowd of ordinary decent folk" and "A million eyes, a million boots in line," while "Old People's Home" (1970) laments a generation "stowed out of conscience / as unpopular luggage."[2] Still, it is primarily the poems of the thirties that recirculate in public discourse today.

To writers of what Samuel Hynes has called "the Auden generation," the 1930s was a time when art could—and must—intervene in social problems. Members of Auden's circle, all Oxbridge educated and all left of center, often crossed class and even national boundaries in their efforts to enlist art with labor and with antifascist movements. In defense of their unapologetic efforts to involve art directly in the issues of their time, Frank Kermode maintains that "it is surely to the credit of the intellectual left, now somewhat despised for *naïveté,* that they were so moved, that they came to believe that they must do something about the whole system that in their view made poverty and war equally inevitable."[3] This was a generation that felt called on to take sides. Like his peers at Oxford, Auden's initiation into labor struggles began with the General Strike of 1926; this event prompted many students to go to London and either drive buses for the government or assist the strikers (Auden drove a car for the Trades Union Congress). When these bourgeois artists began their literary careers in the 1930s, they continued to respond to the working classes. Several writers sought closer contact with workers through documentary projects or through publications aimed across class lines. Auden did both; he collaborated on six documentary films, and he published an essay on poetry for the Workers' Educational Association. The *Daily Worker* became an essential window on contemporary culture even if one did not join the Communist Party, as did Auden's fellow writers Stephen Spender and Cecil Day-Lewis.

When the Spanish Civil War broke out in 1936, the Auden generation was again compelled to take sides—this time on the issue of European fascism. In 1937 Nancy Cunard issued a stark query to the "Writers and Poets" of the British Isles: "Are you for, or against, the legal Government and the People of Republican Spain? Are you for, or against, Franco and Fascism?"[4] One of the signatures on Cunard's query was Auden's; his answer appeared along with twenty-seven others in the *Left Review's* pamphlet, *Authors Take Sides on the Spanish War* (1937). As the decade spiraled toward its catastrophic ending with World War II, the menace of fascism overshadowed the Auden generation's earlier premonitions of class warfare.

Leftist writers who had contended over the artist's role in a future worker's state were now faced with the prospect of total annihilation under a fascist state. German artists forced into exile by the Nazis were arriving in England (Auden married Thomas Mann's daughter Erika, a cabaret artist, to help her acquire a British passport), and Franco's troops executed the writer Federico García Lorca in Spain. Auden's response to Cunard summed up the apprehensions of many British artists: "The spread of Fascist Ideology and practice to countries as yet comparatively free from them, which would inevitably follow upon a Fascist victory in Spain, would create an atmosphere in which the creative artist and all who care for justice, liberty and culture would find it impossible to work or even exist."[5] Just as members of the Auden generation had traveled to Britain's industrial North to gain a better understanding of the working classes and labor issues, they now traveled to Spain to gain firsthand knowledge of the fight against fascism. After his visit there, Auden would join Christopher Isherwood in a journey to China and observe further fascist aggression in the form of Japanese bombers; this journey became the basis of a documentary travelogue. It was no longer enough for poets to be Shelley's "unacknowledged legislators of the World"; the socially engaged artist had to establish contact with the victims of injustice and bear witness to a world in crisis.

For many contemporary assessors, thirties writers' passions and commitments present a stance that seems unfashionable in an era that regards with more suspicion artists' claims about effecting social change. As Seamus Heaney puts it, "no lyric has ever stopped a tank"—an echo of Auden's famous line from his 1939 elegy for Yeats, "For poetry makes nothing happen."[6] Although the occasional issues-oriented anthology enlists poetry in a particular cause (such as *Poets for Life: Seventy-six Poets Respond to AIDS,* 1989), we see fewer examples of interventionist literature than 1930s audiences did. Yet the idea of socially engaged art that was so central to thirties culture remains very much a part of our own.

Words and images from that crisis-ridden time survive as afterimages in cultural memory, such as George Orwell's shocking account of coal miners' living conditions in Wigan Pier and Robert Capa's dramatic photograph of a Republican soldier falling dead in Spain. By reactivating the thirties—often in the context of contemporary issues—these texts' survival enacts the process of cultural work that Auden foresaw in his Yeats elegy:

> For poetry makes nothing happen: it survives
> In the valley of its saying where executives
> Would never want to tamper; it flows south
> From ranches of isolation and the busy griefs,
> Raw towns that we believe and die in; it survives,
> A way of happening, a mouth.

Auden's use of the river trope clarifies the poem's stance on art and social action: he is not saying the two are incompatible. In fact, Auden charts a course for poetry that gradually enlarges its social domain and influence. As the poem enters culture, it leaves the author ("the valley of its saying") for coterie audiences ("ranches of isolation"), then broadens further to reach larger discourse communities ("raw towns"). The fused image that culminates this section of the Yeats elegy evokes both a river's mouth and a human mouth; together they convey a larger social arena that Stan Smith has called "the sea of public discourse."[7] As the work of art moves from poet to public, then, it becomes a conduit through which collective action can take place, "a way of happening." Straddling its own historical conditions and those of its audience, poetry as Auden sees it offers us a way of connecting with others.

THIS BOOK not only examines Auden as an author of literature but also invokes Auden as *a way of thinking* about the 1930s and socially engaged art. A cultural figure that has become synonymous with this vexing decade, the signifier "Auden" exceeds both the person and his texts. His words fuse with ours when we confront social crises, so that at some point "Auden" stops referring *to* the thirties and, in effect, *becomes* them. We can see this confluence in public discourse surrounding two events that have reactivated the 1930s in cultural memory—the fiftieth anniversary of VE Day and the civil war in Bosnia. When quotation marks vanish from the quoted words, as they do in the headlines below, "Auden" has surpassed the domain of literary authorship and entered the culture at large:

> But in the bloody dawning of the post-cold-war world, we see that the issues that underlay World War II confront us still, no easier to answer now, it turns out, than in what the poet Auden fashionably reviled as the "low dishonest decade" of the 1930s. (*Newsweek,* 22 May 1995)

> In the nightmare of the dark
> All the dogs of Europe bark,
> And the living nations wait,
> Each sequestered in its hate.

> That innocent-appearing stanza crops up toward the end of W. H. Auden's poem, "In Memory of W. B. Yeats," composed in 1939, as Europe slid into the steaming maw of war. . . .What Auden wrote over the corpse of Yeats could be said today over Yugoslavia's remains. ("Yugoslavia's Dark Cold Day," *Boston Globe,* 28 November 1991)

> Auden's words on Spain stick in the mind when the meaning of Bosnia's defeat is contemplated. "We are left alone with our day," he wrote, "and the time is short, and / History to the defeated / May say alas but cannot help or pardon." ("Alas, but We Cannot Help or Pardon," *Herald* [Glasgow], 1 June 1995)

Thus the well-known poems "September 1, 1939," "In Memory of W. B. Yeats," and *Spain* leave us a double legacy: they shape cultural memories of the thirties, and they provide strategies for coming to terms with contemporary social conflicts. Edward Mendelson claims that "more than any other," Auden's poetry "contributed to the understanding of his time."[8] Given the ways that contemporary journalists reroute his poems to address Bosnia, Auden may prove equally central in understanding our own time.

Despite the intertwining of Auden and the thirties in cultural memory, two critical trends have recently attempted to wrest the artist and the decade from one another. The first occurs in literary histories that aim to, as Adrian Caesar puts it, "de-centre Auden's place in the 1930s" and thus challenge Hynes's earlier construction of the Auden generation.[9] Caesar's *Dividing Lines: Poetry, Class and Ideology in the 1930s* (1991) adopts the strategy of emphasizing poets and literary magazines outside Auden's circle and *New Verse;* Valentine Cunningham's *British Writers of the Thirties* (1988) surrounds Auden with three generations of writers who published in that decade—including two of his most vehement detractors, Evelyn Waugh and George Orwell. The second trend, which occurs in Auden criticism, aims to decenter the thirties from Auden. Often framing his poems with his own critical essays instead of with socioeconomic contexts, such studies counter those who see Auden's political engagement as the definitive aspect of his career. For example, Lucy McDiarmid's *Auden's Apologies for Poetry* (1990) focuses on the "New York" Auden and his writings about art, claiming that his primary target as a writer was not bourgeois society but literature. John R. Boly's *Reading Auden: The Returns of Caliban* (1991) examines the ways Auden's poems reveal the dynamics of the reading process; although Boly draws several examples from the thirties poems, his interest lies in textual rather than actual events.

My own approach shares the goals of enlarging our understanding of thirties culture and expanding the Auden canon, yet it departs from these critics' frameworks in two important ways. First, my analysis does not question the social engagement of Auden's thirties texts by, on the one hand, supplanting him with writers deemed more "committed" or, on the other, supplanting socioeconomic issues with less politicized ones. Whereas some would justify both positions by pointing to Auden's postthirties disavowals of political action, I would caution against limiting a text's social power to its author's stated beliefs. Instead of continuing the standard debates about Auden's individual politics, I am more interested in examining the politics of thirties representations. In this sense my work is indebted to the emerging field of cultural studies, which, as Patrick Brantlinger points out, "locates the sources of meaning not in individual reason or subjectivity, but in social relations, communication, cultural politics."[10] Second, my domain is not limited to Auden's verbal texts; it restores to his canon the visual texts that he produced alone (his published photographs) and those he produced in collaboration with others (his contributions to documentary filmmaking). Taking this "visual Auden" into account allows us to explore thirties culture's documentary network of literary, photographic, and filmic responses to social crisis.

The thirties survive not only through individual texts, but also through the documentary genre. Like Orwell's miners and Capa's Spanish soldier, many of the period's most enduring images are documentary in nature; the decade that launched the Auden generation is also the decade that established documentary discourse as our century's principal means of representing social reality. Filmmaker John Grierson both introduced the word "documentary" to British culture and founded what would become the largest center of documentary production in the thirties. By organizing Britain's first government-sponsored Film Unit at the Empire Marketing Board (E.M.B.) in 1927, Grierson formed a network of documentary filmmakers and trainees that would expand the Unit's ostensible purpose of promoting empire products to British consumers. As Paul Swann points out, Grierson's innovations with bookkeeping enlarged his staff by contracting unofficial employees to affiliated film companies. These additional productions allowed documentary film to broaden its domain and depict not only a wider range of workers and industry, but also an array of social concerns; during the Film Unit's government sponsorship at the General Post Office (G.P.O., 1933–39), members of Grierson's group produced *Housing Problems, The Smoke Menace,* and *Enough to Eat* for the gas industry. The work of the E.M.B. and G.P.O. Film Units, along with that of Grierson's associates at other film agencies, would become known as the British documentary film movement. In his study of Grierson, Ian Aitken has noted the thematic parallels these documentarists shared with Auden and his literary circle: a preference for "industrial subject matter," a sense that the depression revealed capitalism's failures, and a belief in artistic commitment.[11]

Auden made significant contributions to the General Post Office Film Unit during his six months' employment in 1935 and 1936. His colleague Paul Rotha, a filmmaker who was also the British documentary movement's major historian and theorist, acknowledged Auden's importance in "introduc[ing] poetry into film speech," noting that poetic narration might provide a welcome counterpart to documentary film's "conventional method of the professional commentator."[12] *Night Mail* (1936), the most famous G.P.O. production, made innovative use of Auden's verse in its culminating sequence; the film depicts a postal train's nightly run from London to Glasgow.

Auden also collaborated on five other documentary films for the G.P.O. Film Unit and its affiliates. His first project, *Coal Face* (1935), examines the British coal mining industry; it received a medal at the 1935 International Film Festival. *Beside the Sea Side* (1935) and *The Way to the Sea* (1937) promote tourism in their respective portrayals of a coastal community and a new electric railway from London to Southampton. *The Londoners* (1939) marks the London City Council's Jubilee celebration, while *God's Chillun* (1939) explores the impact of Europe's slave trade on the Caribbean. In addition to writing commentaries, Auden occasionally served as directorial assistant and learned how films were edited. He also gave a brief lecture titled "Poetry and Film" to the North London Film Society in 1936, thus participating in the documentary film movement's promotion of its new art form. Yet Auden's relationship to documentary representation involves broader cultural parameters than his employment at the G.P.O. Film Unit.

A second center of documentary activity in Britain was the Mass-Observation movement, cofounded in 1937 by the G.P.O. filmmaker Humphrey Jennings, the poet Charles Madge, and the anthropologist Tom Harrisson. This collective used an array of human observers to record their own and others' behavior; the latter might include such assignments as "Behaviour of people at war memorials" and "Female taboos about eating." Although Mass-Observation's interest in public—or "mass"—identity departed from the scope of Grierson's film units, both documentary movements shared the Auden generation's fascination with Britain's working classes. Auden did not participate in this documentary movement, although *Letters from Iceland* bequeaths to Madge "some curious happenings to correlate."[13] As we shall see, Auden shaped, reflected, and interrogated documentary representation not only through his film work, but also through his poetry, essays, dispatches, photographs, and documentary travelogues.

IN THIS book I read Auden and documentary *through one another,* revising the one-way dynamic of the traditional influence study in which an artistic movement casts light on a writer's work. Several of Auden's texts employ documentary frameworks while calling those frameworks into question. For example, the poem "Who stands, the crux left of the watershed" ("The Watershed") participates in documentary's sustained act of looking across class lines, yet it also questions the documentary observer's presence in the industrial scene. Positioned on the threshold of the thirties and Auden's canon, "The Watershed" offers a good starting point for reading documentary discourse through Auden. This poem, first published in 1928, appeared in his debut Faber volume, *Poems* (1930), and it is often the initial Auden selection in modern poetry anthologies.

"The Watershed" surveys an industrial landscape through a double act of looking; we perceive the scene through a stranger who enters unfamiliar territory and through the poem's disembodied speaker who observes this stranger's activity. At first glance, the landscape appears decayed and depopulated, an appropriate scene for expressing modernist alienation:

> Who stands, the crux left of the watershed,
> On the wet road between the chafing grass
> Below him sees dismantled washing-floors,
> Snatches of tramline running to the wood,
> An industry already comatose,
> Yet sparsely living. A ramshackle engine
> At Cashwell raises water; for ten years
> It lay in flooded workings until this,
> Its latter office, grudgingly performed . . .[14]

But we should also note that some of this machinery still operates (the "ramshackle engine"); in fact, the landscape's "comatose" industry is still "sparsely living." The latter phrase means not only "barely alive," the usual gloss, but also the struggle of living frugally in the developing depression. This socioeconomic marker shows that the poem's terrain is more than the psychological projection that Mendelson and others have seen. As I shall discuss in the next chapter, Auden's industrial landscapes reflect his culture's documentary excursions into the working-class communities of Britain's North.

Significantly, miners occupy the center of "The Watershed":

> . . . two there were
> Cleaned out a damaged shaft by hand, clutching
> The winch the gale would tear them from; one died
> During a storm, the fells impassable,
> Not at his village, but in wooden shape
> Through long abandoned levels nosed his way
> And in his final valley went to ground.

All three of these workers died in mines. The "wooden shape" in "long abandoned levels" is not only a coffin—the gloss Katherine Bucknell offers in *Juvenilia*—but also the support beams that once held the tunnel ceilings in place. Auden's death scenes do more than enhance the poem's ominous tone; they also point to the dangers miners faced during Britain's depression. As Noreen Branson and Margot Heinemann explain, "Standards of roof support and safety suffered in the drive for low-cost output," and the noise of mechanical cutters "made it harder to hear cracks in the timber."[15]

The documentary observers who traveled through mining country in the 1930s were also struck by deplorable working conditions. J. B. Priestley's *English Journey* (1934), the G.P.O. Film Unit's *Coal Face* (1935), and Orwell's *The Road to Wigan Pier* (1937) all cite alarming statistics of the number of coal miners killed on the job. According to Priestley, for example, "During the five years ending with 1931 more than 5,000 people were killed in the coal-mining industry, and more than 800,000 people injured"; the composition of "The Watershed" falls within this historical period. *English Journey*'s account of how these miners die is especially horrific:" Every man or boy who goes underground knows only too well that he risks one of several peculiarly horrible deaths, from being roasted to being imprisoned in the rock and slowly suffocated."[16] Mirroring documentary's discrepancies between economic and iconographic power, those who bear the brunt of Britain's labor struggles are also those who energize Auden's poem.

Auden's modernist predecessors Wilfred Owen and D. H. Lawrence provide additional contexts for the images of mining accidents in "The Watershed." Auden's juvenilia poems of the industrial North—especially "The Miner's Wife"—reveal a heavy debt to Lawrence. But documentary representations of miners departed from these earlier literary influences by employing the statistical language of fact, by emphasizing physical contact with the industrial North, and by focusing more closely on miner's bodies. While traditional literary contexts are important for understanding the cultural dynamics of Auden's poem, documentary contexts are crucial.

The central position of miners marks only one of the documentary aspects of "The Watershed"; the poem's addressee who enters industrial Britain bears striking similarities to documentary observers in thirties texts. His intrusive gaze prompts the poem's opening query, as well as its dramatic imperatives that appear just after the scenes of mining accidents:

> Go home, now, stranger, proud of your young stock,
> Stranger, turn back again, frustrate and vexed:
> This land, cut off, will not communicate . . .

Auden's repeated word "stranger" marks the socioeconomic divide that separates the middle-class observer (and reader) from the North Country's working-class inhabitants. Embarking on "an adventure of observation," Grierson's phrase for the documentary enterprise, Auden's stranger has traveled to a culturally coded terrain that is unfamiliar to him personally. Priestley spoke for many documentary observers when he began his account of the Black Country's industrial terrain with these words: "This *notorious* region was *strange* to me. *Now I have seen it,* but of course it is still *strange* to me." Similarly, Orwell writes that "when you go to the industrial North you are conscious, quite apart from the unfamiliar scenery, of entering *a strange country.*"[17] In all three cases, industrial Britain's notoriety as Britain's other country is precisely what draws the observers' scrutiny and directs their vision, so that firsthand accounts mirror cultural expectations of "strangeness."

Connoting a dark inscrutability as well as grime and soot, the industrial North signified Britain's own heart of darkness—a remote interior where the working-class rituals of work and home were performed. Grierson, in fact, would link documentary film's explorations of the industrial North to earlier British explorations of Africa: "Our gentlemen explore the native haunts and investigate the native customs of Tanganyika and Timbuctoo, but do not travel dangerously into the jungles of Middlesbrough and the Clyde." This imperialist construction of working-class communities as colonial territories has precedents in the Victorian urban exploration narratives that Judith R. Walkowitz has assessed, in which London's affluent West End and impoverished East End "imaginatively doubled for England and its Empire." Of course industrial Britain did not appear exotic or strange to those who lived and labored there; as Smith notes in his comments on "The Watershed," bourgeois social construction can cause one to see "through a class darkly."[18]

While Auden's poem intersects with thirties documentary practice, it also pressures emerging documentary conventions in ways that suggest alternatives. In this context, the line "This land, cut off, will not communicate" signifies not an *inability* to communicate, but a *refusal* to serve as what Mendelson calls "accessory content" to bourgeois representations, such as the "tourist's inventory of places seen"—or documentary texts. The poem's taunting speaker becomes the voice of industrial Britain wresting interpretive control from the voice-over narration that usually accompanies documentary images of mines and miners. As William Stott writes of American documentary, the genre aimed to "giv[e] the inarticulate a voice"[19]—an enterprise blind to the representational inequality that positions one class as mute and the other as articulate, one class before the camera and one behind it. In "The Watershed," inarticulateness becomes a deliberate strategy for thwarting easy access to Britain's industrial North; the poem's intruding stranger—and the reader—must *work* these notoriously cryptic passages to render them legible. Turning what John Tagg calls "the axis of representation" back on the middle classes, the poem's speaker leaves the miners' bodies hidden and exposes the stranger's presence. Moreover, the poem's imperatives ("Go home," "turn back") expel this observer from the scene; he is denied the visual authority that conventional documentaries depend on. The alternative dynamics of "The Watershed" allow space for critiquing representation—a feature that runs across the spectrum of Auden's documentary work.

THIRTIES DOCUMENTARY practice linked together filmmakers, photographers, and writers in a largely male network. Besides Auden's G.P.O. colleagues Grierson and Rotha, I also bring into this book's framework filmmaker Joris Ivens and combat photographer Robert Capa. In addition to Priestley and Orwell, I discuss writers Charles Madge, Ernest Hemingway, Christopher Isherwood, and Peter Fleming. These documentary observers interacted physically, textually, and culturally to construct a discourse of reality that could represent the social crises of a decade that began with an economic depression and ended at the brink of global war. As it emerged in the thirties, documentary expression responded to these and other crises that unsettled relations of gender, sexuality, class, and nationality.

In assessing Auden's relation to documentary, this book reconsiders well-known texts (*Night Mail, Spain*) and recovers critically neglected ones (*Letters from Iceland, Journey to a War*); the latter have become available again through Paragon House. Chapters 2 and 4 locate cultural networks around major focal points for thirties documentary—the working classes of Britain's industrial North and the war against fascism in Spain, respectively. Chapters 3 and 5 offer extended readings of Auden photo-texts that suggest alternatives to conventional documentary practice.

Chapter 2 interrogates representations of Britain's industrial workers to assess the masculinity of thirties documentary discourse. Although the images of workers by Auden and the British documentary film movement have generated much critical controversy, these discussions often lose sight of both the plurality of the working classes and the gendering of documentary practice. The chapter considers rival constructions of male industrial workers—the craftsman and the coal miner—in Auden's industrial poems, his essays about labor, J. B. Priestley's *English Journey,* George Orwell's *The Road to Wigan Pier,* and the documentary films *Industrial Britain, Coal Face,* and *Night Mail.* This intersection of Auden, documentary, and the thirties invites us to revise Laura Mulvey's influential theory of the male gaze to account for the dynamics of documentary representation, which often employed a male-on-male gaze. As Bill Nichols notes, in documentary cinema "the camera's gaze can still be treated as gendered and fully implicated in questions of desire as well as control."[20] By acknowledging what Eve Kosofsky Sedgwick would call the "homosocial" structure of thirties documentary practice, we can see that gender and sexuality—as well as class—shaped this emerging form of representation in Britain.

In Chapter 3 I read *Letters from Iceland,* an experimental phototext written in collaboration with Louis MacNeice, as an early example of self-reflexive documentary form. Produced shortly after Auden left the G.P.O. Film Unit, this book offers an extended response to the representational strategies of the documentary film movement; it also marks the first publication of Auden's photographs. By combining the populism of thirties documentary and the fragmentation of high modernist collage, *Letters from Iceland* attempts to achieve a more socially conscious, less aggressive gaze than either form can produce alone. This "public collage" subverts the visual authority of both discourses by blurring boundaries between observer and observed. Auden's photographs prove crucial to this agenda; while some of them emulate conventional documentary framings, others fragment their subjects with jarring angles. Organizing these competing visual and verbal texts into a cohesive whole becomes a deliberately impossible task for Auden and his readers. *Letters from Iceland* anticipates features that Paul Arthur has noted in contemporary documentary practice: it interrogates the prospect of completing "a straightforward documentary project," and it employs an "unprecedented degree of hybridization."[21]

Chapter 4 places Auden's poem *Spain* in an extended dialogue with two visual texts of the Spanish Civil War to consider alternative models of artistic intervention. Like *Spain,* the American documentary film *The Spanish Earth* and Robert Capa's photograph of a Republican soldier's death dominate our cultural memory of the Spanish conflict. Whereas conventional criticism would deem these front-line, documentary texts as more "engaged" than Auden's often distanced and abstract poem, this assumption ignores the ways all three pro-Republican texts revise common conceptions of committed leftist art. Adopting Popular Front strategies, *Spain* and *The Spanish Earth* eschew partisan labels and an anchoring, testimonial voice to construct discursive democracies that elicit the audience's participation. This avoidance of inflammatory rhetoric enabled each text to fulfill its role as a fund-raiser on behalf of Republican medical aid. *Spain* shares different representational strategies with Capa's news photograph; both decontextualize their framing in ways that allow these texts to address subsequent wars while still preserving the Spanish conflict in cultural memory. Because of *Spain's* ability to both intervene in its historical moment and offer us strategies for confronting current global conflicts, it has become one of the Spanish Civil War's most frequently invoked heuristic devices.

My concluding chapter examines *Journey to a War*—Auden's final documentary text—as a self-reflective work that exposes not only the compromised position of its authors, but also the contradictions of British documentary practice. Produced in collaboration with Christopher Isherwood, this book of prose, poetry, and Auden's photographs effects an extended confrontation between documentary discourse and the genre's heterosexist and colonialist genealogy. I read the book's title as a double emplotment that signifies both a literal and a metaphoric "journey." Literally, Auden and Isherwood travel to China so they can reach the front of the Sino-Japanese War and capture it in their text, thus fulfilling the role of documentary men. But in seeking the elusive front, these gay Englishmen must negotiate competing models of masculinity and mediating signs of European colonialism. Metaphorically, *Journey to a War*'s excursions into China enact British documentary's return to its imperialist origins in the Empire Marketing Board—a confrontation that exposes the "fronts" of documentary discourse. In discussing Auden and Isherwood's self-scrutinizing text, this chapter revisits the book's major issues—documentary's unacknowledged masculinity, its authoritative structure, and its Popular Front interventions.

More than any other image-making practice, documentary exposes the contest of meanings within the word "representation." Because it carries a legislative as well as a signifying sense, "to represent" implies that in portraying an underemployed laborer or a war refugee, one also speaks or acts on behalf of that person. This double meaning has proved problematic for documentary's practitioners and critics, fueling debates about whether it can provide social advocacy across class lines or national boundaries. In her recent account of American documentary, Paula Rabinowitz speaks urgently of the need to understand and then rework the power relations of traditional documentary practice: "Without a radical break from the regimes of vision and narrative we will only see and write with the eyes and hands of those who have already looked us over and described what they've seen (of) themselves." And in his reassessment of the British documentary film tradition, Brian Winston calls for a "rescue" of the genre that would launch a "Post-Griersonian Documentary."[22] Auden's vexed engagement with documentary representation shows that some of the tools for reinventing the genre might lie within alternative models from the 1930s. By initiating a generative recovery from the decade that continues to provide our dominant models of socially engaged art, we might carry forward their experiments in ways we have yet to imagine.

2

DOCUMENTARY AND MASCULINITY

Auden and "the Worker"
of Industrial Britain

REPRESENTATIONS OF workers have gener-
ated the greatest critical controversies over the thirties texts of both
W. H. Auden and the British documentary film movement. Curiously,
most critics who address Auden's images of workers ignore his collaborations with documentary filmmakers who aimed to bring more
workmen's portraits to the screen. For example, the same double
issue of *New Verse* (1937) that deemed Auden "revolutionary" also
contained Allen Tate's stinging remark that Auden has "discovered
that people work in factories and mines," but "instead of finding out
about them" writes "poems calling them Comrades from a distance."
In fact, Auden's first project with the G.P.O. Film Unit—a documentary about mining called *Coal Face*—screened a year before Tate's re-
buke. Yet despite documentary film's vantage point closer to workers,
the productions of John Grierson's E.M.B. and G.P.O. Film Units have
stimulated critical debates that parallel those surrounding Auden's
poems. For example, while Erik Barnouw asserts that the G.P.O. Film
Unit's *Coal Face* "sounded a note of protest and of urgent need for reform," Peter Miles and Malcolm Smith counter that "it would certainly be difficult" to label this film "in any sense radical from the political point of view."[1]

Typically, critics assess Auden's and the filmmakers' images of
workers to determine whether these bourgeois artists meet the Marxist demand of "going over" to the proletariat in their texts, concluding that they are either progressive or conservative. Guided by the
question, "How does documentary representation frame the worker?"
such debates have rightly prompted us to interrogate documentarists'

16

often unreflective defenses of their work. Yet this kind of criticism often limits our understanding of thirties representations in two ways. First, it locates the primary impetus of meaning within the artists themselves; second, it grants documentarists too much power by ignoring the ways images of workers can disrupt the documentary frame. For as literary and filmic representations reveal, the men who labored in Britain's industrial North were a diverse group, and they triggered enormous cultural anxieties in documentary texts.

In the 1930s, Britain's industrial workers faced the impact of the new mass production employee on the traditional division of trade unions into craftsmen's and laborers' unions. So we must question the unitary term "the worker"—a staple of both the decade's discourse and retrospective criticism on documentary representation. Upon examination, each key word proves to be much more unstable than this seemingly definitive phrase suggests.

First, we must bear in mind that thirties writers relied heavily on the definite article—a feature that critics have noted in Auden's early poetry. As Valentine Cunningham has asserted, the decade's widespread literary use of "the" was "an effort to assert authority, knowledge, command of experience, the capacity to muster typologies." Because many perceived this time as a perpetual state of crisis, the desire to contain social reality is hardly surprising. The same authoritative discourse would characterize the voice-over narration of documentary films; invisible commentators imparted socioeconomic information about "the industrial towns," "the craftsman," and "the miner." David Trotter's characterization of the effect the definite article has on Auden's poetry reveals the instability lurking beneath its appearance of control: this part of speech "relies on the reader to complete the identification" because it "has no semantic content and does not position the individual or sub-class it refers to."[2] So which worker are we to visualize when we encounter the protean term "the worker"? Although it usually eliminates white-collar workers from consideration, there remain such divergent groups as skilled, semi-skilled, and unskilled workers, each with a different form and degree of organization. Thus we should ask which labor group(s) and issues a critic means when he or she pronounces that a writer, filmmaker, or text lacks commitment to "the worker."

Besides its tendency to collapse working-class particularities and differences into homogeneous categories, "the worker" proves problematic in a second way by obscuring the user's political stance and affiliation. In this sense the noun also contributes to the phrase's vexing fluidity. Consider, for example, the recurrence of "the worker" in prominent leftist media organizations of the 1930s—such as the *Daily Worker* and the Workers' Film and Photo League. Does "worker" mean that these organizations' respective representations are *produced by* workers, *produced for* workers, or *produced on behalf of* workers, or simply that they are *about* workers? These interpretive choices each hold vastly different political implications, so that conflating two or more of them can prompt hasty assumptions detrimental to our understanding of Auden, documentary, and the thirties.

As with the decade's reliance on the definite article, its dependence on the catchall term "worker" was an attempt to contain social flux— a maneuver that is most apparent in the call for "going over to the worker." Positioning the working classes as a fixed, unitary destination, the "going over" model belies its egalitarian claims by assigning freedom of choice and movement to the bourgeoisie—a contradiction that also vexes documentary representation. Yet the figure of the worker would rest uneasily within these discursive boundaries. Even if "going over" were a two-way street, the would-be fellow traveler would still face the dilemma of choosing the "representative" worker from such divergent groups as dockworkers, bus drivers, coal miners, craft workers, textile workers, and factory operatives. Given this linguistic fluidity of "the worker," then, it is not surprising that images of workers often disrupted the decade's documentary framings.

Two fixed points gave some anchorage to the discursive existence of "the worker" so that representational networks could form in thirties culture. First, documentary usually staged the figure of "the worker" in Britain's industrial North; second, thirties discourse almost invariably gendered this worker as male. Using these compass points, the following chapter assesses rival constructions of the male industrial worker in documentary representation. Images of the craftsman, a surrogate artist figure, reflected cultural anxieties about being an "individual," while images of the coal miner, a sexualized other, reflected anxieties about being a "man." My analysis draws its examples from these key texts of the thirties: Auden's essays about labor, his industrial poems, J. B. Priestley's *English Journey,* George

Orwell's *The Road to Wigan Pier*, and the British documentary film movement's *Industrial Britain* and *Coal Face*. I also discuss the documentary film movement's eventual repression of the industrial North in *Night Mail*, Auden's best-known collaboration with the G.P.O. Film Unit. By showing that gender and sexuality—as well as class—fueled the sense of social and representational crisis in Britain, this chapter examines standard assumptions about Auden and the documentary film movement.

Mapping Britain's Industrial North

Male writers, filmmakers and photographers traveled north to Britain's industrial regions during the 1930s, a cultural convergence that attested not only to this terrain's prominence in literary and visual media, but also to documentary's growing influence. The Mass-Observation collective even established a second headquarters in the industrial town of Bolton so members could have continuous access to a working-class community. Like London's male urban explorers of the late Victorian period, thirties documentary observers transgressed class lines to establish contact with the working classes. Both examples of bourgeois scrutiny mixed class voyeurism and social reformism, a vexed dynamic that Judith R. Walkowitz has assessed in Victorian accounts of London's "other" city. Yet the greater physical distance involved in traveling to the North Country—as opposed to nightwalking London's slums—coalesced with the decade's central metaphor of "going over" to distinguish the documentary observer's ostensible desire to learn from—rather than instruct—the worker. Despite documentary's extensive travels into working-class terrain, the growing repertoire of public images shaped representation as much as did actual encounters with the industrial North. For example, filmmaker Paul Rotha and photographer Bill Brandt both acknowledged the influence of Priestley's *English Journey* on their respective texts, *The Face of Britain* (1935) and *The English at Home* (1936). This intersection of actual and textual territory riddled documentary's map of thirties industrial Britain.

Geographically, the industrial North includes Lancashire (the district of both Bolton and Orwell's *Wigan Pier*), the West and East Ridings of Yorkshire (Priestley grew up in the former), Wearside, and Tyneside. Yet Philip Dodd explains that this region "is less a number of particular places with specific histories" than a "place with an agreed iconography." Thus the industrial Britain of the thirties included not only the mining districts of the Midlands (the region of Birmingham—Auden's hometown—and the Black Country), but also those of South Wales. Rather than indicating a particular geographical direction, then, Britain's "North" designates an economic margin to London's center. This figurative existence of industrial Britain explains why the publishers of *The Road to Wigan Pier* could include photographs of squalor far from the mining community Orwell visited—including collieries in South Wales, miners' shacks in Newcastle, and even slums within London itself. In the visual text of *Wigan Pier,* also indebted to *English Journey,* the grimy slag heaps and decrepit buildings spill over the North's border to threaten England's center, a textual proliferation illustrating Peter Stallybrass and Allon White's contention that "what is *socially* peripheral is so frequently *symbolically* central."[3] We might think of thirties industrial Britain as a metaphoric black country that animates and unsettles documentary representation.

Just as not all of industrial Britain appeared due north of London, neither did all of it suffer economic decline. John Stevenson points out that while the 1930s was "a period of prolonged depression in the old staple industries" such as coal production, the decade also marked "the time when a new industrial structure" based on electric power "provided the real basis for the export boom and the rising prosperity of the second half of the twentieth century." Because of this shift in industrial production, the economic gap between classes widened considerably. Mass consumption of electrical home appliances attested to the middle class's growing economic prosperity, but as Noreen Branson and Margot Heinemann assert, "There can be no doubt at all that employed miners, even at the end of the thirties, were living worse than they had done before the First World War."[4]

Drawn to such areas of industrial decline, documentary discourse defined the "real" industrial Britain as the poverty-stricken regions bearing the brunt of the depression.[5] Stallybrass and White discuss such discrepancies in economic and iconographic power, asserting that though "the low-Other is despised and denied at the level of political organization and social being," it nonetheless proves "instrumentally constitutive of the shared imaginary repertoires of the dominant culture."[6] In the case of thirties documentary practice, the economically marginalized black countries became a rugged testing ground for "real men" who triggered bourgeois male identification and desire.

Documentary and "Real" Men

Thirties documentary practice gendered industrial Britain as almost exclusively male even though, as Stevenson points out, the number of female workers actually rose in the light industries. Documentary framings of the North conventionally render women invisible or relegate them to domestic space; Robert Colls and Philip Dodd correctly note that "working-class women are simply read out of the picture or 'left' at home."[7] The E.M.B. film *Industrial Britain* goes so far as to expel women from its frame. Although its opening sequence contains brief shots of two women working (one at a spinning wheel, the other at a loom), the male voice-over labels them "scenes of yesterday"; in other words, women's labor belongs to the preindustrial order.[8] (The shot of the second woman, who faces away from the camera, reinforces this expulsion.) Even the G.P.O. film *Coal Face*, with its innovative women's chorus written by Auden, shows them only metonymically—in a brief shot of a laundry-laden clothesline marking the miners' return home. Generally speaking, then, "woman" figured into industrial Britain as "not work" and thus not the primary material of documentary representation.

This male gendering of the industrial North marked another departure from cross-class spectatorship in Victorian London, where, as Walkowitz states, "the [female] prostitute was a central spectacle in a set of urban encounters and fantasies." It also departs from the Victorian diaries and photographs of Alfred J. Munby, whose fascination with women laborers—including miners—hinges on gender as well as class difference. Although Paula Rabinowitz finds Munby's project central to documentary's "slippage between class power and sexual knowledge," we must note the male-male dynamic that shaped documentary images of industrial workers in the thirties.[9]

With its erected chimneys and penetrating mines, industrial Britain was masculine terrain. Moreover, documentary's worker not only was male, he was a "real" man, and thus a point of identification for the male documentarist and his male readers and viewers. Craftsmen possessed capable bodies that performed with sureness and skill, while coal miners—the most "manly" workers—had muscular bodies that performed with strength and endurance. So documentarists who entered Britain's metaphoric black country also confronted their own status as physically inferior men. Traditionally, the cultural configuration of Britain's industrial North combines a body/mind dualism with bifurcations along gender as well as class lines; Dodd explains that "the North is masculine, working class and physical; the South, feminine, middle-class and spiritual." Orwell confronts this dividing line in the self-examination that follows his accounts of coal miners in *The Road to Wigan Pier.* Faced with the "accusation" that "because I have been to a public school I am a eunuch," he writes, "I can produce medical evidence to the contrary, but what good will that do?"[10] So the male documentarist faced a dilemma: How could he represent industrial workers without calling into question his own masculinity?

Documentary observers employed various strategies for erasing the North/South divide that threatened to unman them. One strategy for closing the distance between their own manhood and the workers' was to use their sustained contact with industrial Britain to call attention to the documentarist's position as a man among real men. In the documentary section of *Wigan Pier,* for example, Orwell shows his grit by shifting to second-person pronouns in his account of descending into coal mines: "When you crawl out at the bottom you are perhaps four hundred yards under ground. That is to say you have a tolerable-sized mountain on top of you." Orwell also wants his male reader to know that he is no mine tourist, but an initiate who merits admiration. Listen to the tough swagger of this assertion: "When you have been down two or three pits you begin to get some grasp of the processes that are going on underground." Assuming that his readers have *not* descended mines, Orwell displaces the "pang of envy" that he feels for miners' "toughness" onto his male readers; they are to envy Orwell's toughness by association.[11] In other words, the uninitiated man replaces the documentarist's former position on the "eunuch" side of the line.

Such hypermasculine coding of industrial Britain was so deep that Auden did not need to write a first-person account of mine shafts to activate its conferral of manliness, although growing up in Birmingham gave him a northern aura. In the same year that *Wigan Pier* was published, the detractors and defenders contributing to *New Verse*'s Auden Double Number agreed on this: they linked his writing to the industrial North and the working classes, and they gendered it as strongly male. For example, George Barker cites Auden's "cocksureness" as a technical "danger," while Bernard Spencer pronounces with approval, "Auden doesn't go soft."[12]

Another documentary strategy pushed this transfer of masculinity further by gendering the genre itself. Rotha, who collaborated with Grierson at the E.M.B. and G.P.O. Film Units, claimed that "the documentary method" is "the most *virile* of all kinds of film." His account of the new genre, *Documentary Film* (1936), renders strategic camera angles into "weapons with which the director fights to put across his theme." Grierson also invoked an aggressive masculinity in his defenses of the British documentary film movement, casting his group of filmmakers as commandos of the documentary aesthetic. For example, in 1937 he boasted of "the documentary men . . . fighting synthetic nonsense," and in 1939 he hailed them as "taking command" in a "Battle for Authenticity." By contrast, Grierson characterized commercial cinema as "impotent and self-conscious art." Thus documentary practice became a male enterprise, and a commitment to portraying the real men of Britain's industrial North became an assertion of masculinity.

We can still see the effects of this male gendering in postmodern American films as diverse as Michael Moore's *Roger and Me* (which maintains documentary's traditional focus on workers) and Ross McElwee's *Sherman's March* (which departs from it). As Bill Nichols asserts, the documentarists' goals in these films—"to save the community, to find a mate"—replicate the "classic goals for male fiction heroes."[13] Examining thirties representations of male workers helps us to reassess the role of gender in documentary history because these images present competing models of masculinity.

Documenting the Craftsman

Although he does not shape our afterimages of the thirties, the craftsman was an important figure in the decade's early constructions of the industrial North. Extended portrayals of craft labor appeared in documentary texts several years before the G.P.O. Film Unit's *Coal Face* and Orwell's *The Road to Wigan Pier* focused the genre's scrutiny on coal miners. Craftsmen's unions remained a dominant form of labor organization during this time (laborers' unions being the other). And contrary to their Victorian predecessors, thirties craft unions were often militant; as Branson and Heinemann point out, "While in the nineteenth century the craft unions had been the centre of conservative ideas and the unskilled unions the focus of socialism, in the thirties the general workers' unions usually constituted the main strength of the right." Yet there are some Victorian precedents for documentary's valuation of the craftsman as an individual worker whose artistry distinguished him from what Auden called the "mass of unskilled workers for whom their real life must lie outside their employment."[14] Like John Ruskin and William Morris, thirties documentarists saw in the high-quality, handcrafted product a reflection of a manly life that integrated mind and body. But whereas these Victorian thinkers constructed craft workers as needing gentlemanly instruction to become whole men, documentarists such as Priestley constructed them as possessing the physical dexterity of real men.

Shaping pottery and glass by hand, etching them with simple tools, industrial Britain's craftsmen seemed a still center in a rapidly changing world. Even in the more modern, nondecorative applications of craft labor—such as porcelain for electrical fittings or colored glass for signal lamps—middle-class observers saw one of society's few remaining occupations that, as Auden would put it in 1939, "really demand[s] the full exercise of the individual's powers." His 1933 essay "How to Be Masters of the Machine" articulates the decade's anxiety about the growth of mass production. Besides job security, Auden argues that what people "really want" is "to do something, to make things, to discover new facts, prove to yourself and others by your skill or brains that you are worth something, in fact, to give your existence a material meaning." Yet in an increasingly mechanized environment where alienated labor replaced satisfying work, he found individual growth thwarted. His poem "The Capital," written in 1938, decries "Factories where lives are made for a temporary use / Like collars or chairs," while his essay for the *I Believe* anthology asserts that "most people are being degraded by the work they do." In short, many in the Auden generation believed that modern factories manufactured the unindividuated mass worker as well as undistinguished mass goods, echoing Ruskin's earlier perception that industrialization yielded the "degradation of the operative into a machine."[15]

By contrast, the craftsman offered an idealized image of individual labor in the thirties, especially through the documentary genre. For example, Priestley's characterization of craft labor in *English Journey* contends that unlike "*most people* . . .who have to leave their personalities behind as they 'clock in,'" craftsmen can "become more themselves, enlarge their personalities, just because it is here that they can use their skill and find an outlet for their zest." Priestley shares Ruskin's—and Morris's—sense that workers should be able to take creative pleasure in their labor; but notice how the threat of mechanized anonymity spills over the class border in this thirties text. Ruskin's "The Savageness of Gothic Architecture" (in *The Stones of Venice*) often reinforced the class divide by employing paternalistic rhetoric to separate the gentlemanly reader from the working-class men under discussion. In prescribing "what *we* have to do with all *our* laborers," for example, Ruskin put this "stern choice" before his fellow class members: "*You* must either make a tool of the *creature*, or a man of him."[16] Safely contained within class boundaries of self and other, Ruskin and his peers never faced the prospect of degrading work. For Ruskin and his successor Morris, the contemporary craft worker was a diminished figure compared with his medieval predecessor; thus he needed the guidance of artistic-minded gentlemen to regain his former dignity. Documentary's craftsman reveals a more permeable boundary between self and other that reflects the observers' anxieties about the spread of mass culture. For Priestley and Auden, craftsmen prompted middle-class envy because "most people" who earned their living faced the impersonality of clocking in.

Two accounts of the industrial North from the early 1930s—the E.M.B. Film Unit's *Industrial Britain* (1933) and Priestley's *English Journey* (1934)—pressure documentary's class line through the central figure of the individuated craftsman. Departing from the decade's collective images of workers, documentary images of craftsmen show them collaborating with one another in ways that allow for individual creativity and skill. Both the film and the book present distinct work *portraits* of craft workers that differ from images of coal miners presented en masse.

1. Glass craftsman from *Industrial Britain* (E.M.B. Film Unit, 1933). (Courtesy Kino Video)

In *Industrial Britain*'s glassmaking sequence, for example, the camera stays fairly close to each craftsman (usually medium shot to close-up range), so that shots rarely allow the background to dominate the human figure (fig. 1). Framing and lighting often draw the viewer's attention to these workers' faces, whose expressions connote a steady concentration (fig. 2).

The film devotes considerable screen time to the senior glass craftsman shown here, introducing him as "Tim Huckleby, king of the goblet-makers." While we watch him at work, the voice-over individuates this "chairman in the glass world" even further, pointing out that he "started work at twelve and has been making fine goblets these forty years." (The next segment, which depicts a goblet engraver, also names the craftsman and summarizes his background.) Huckleby's name and family history distinguish him from documentary's more typical presentations of workers as representative types, and the narration's epithets "king" and "chairman" elevate him above the common laborer. *English Journey* does not go into *Industrial*

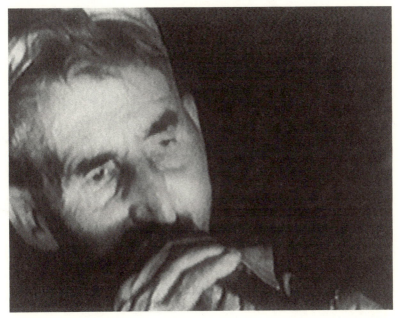

2. Close-up of glass craftsman from *Industrial Britain*. (Courtesy Kino Video)

Britain's level of detail in depicting Potteries craftsmen, yet Priestley often designates individual workers such as the man "performing the difficult operation of 'throwing' large meat dishes," or the "very experienced and highly-skilled man" who "did the turning and decoration of the more important pieces."[17]

By contrast, both texts employ more generalized language in referring to coal miners; the film narration uses the pronoun "they" even if only one miner is shown, while Priestley relies on the definite article ("the miner") and the generic "he." The film and the book also quote statistics to portray miners, an impersonal technique that neither uses in depicting craftsmen. In sum, neither text pits bourgeois individualism against working-class anonymity in its representations of craftsmen; this network of images complicates assumptions that thirties documentarists always constructed "worker" as "other."

Besides pressuring the individual/worker opposition, the images of craftsmen in *Industrial Britain and English Journey* also unsettle another class-inflected binarism that rendered the North legible in the

1930s—"mind/body." These documentary texts stress both aspects of industrial craftsmen's labor, portraying their work as what Auden calls "a real job, needing all their faculties of body and mind." Departing from Victorian predecessors such as Morris, who characterized the "journey-man's work" of wool dyeing as "hard for the body and easy for the mind," Grierson's film and Priestley's book describe craft labor with adjectives denoting mental acumen. For example, *Industrial Britain's* narration praises "the *keen* eyes of the individual" that join with "the hands of a craftsman" to give British products their quality. Similarly, Priestley writes that craftsmen are not "sullen robots" but men whose "*sharp*" eyes proved as crucial to their work as their capable bodies; he also characterizes their activities as "work demanding personal skill and quick *judgment*." Compare these descriptions with *Industrial Britain's* image of a crane operator who "does not think of the world he builds in the course of his daily work" but "perform[s] one of the essential jobs in the making of girders." Unlike the commentary from the film's craft sequence, this excerpt from the steelmaking sequence reinforces class division by assigning mental activity to the bourgeois narrator and viewer; the crane operator becomes simply "a hand on a lever." Thus we must complicate Robert Colls and Philip Dodd's critique of the British documentary film movement, which asserts that the male worker in *Industrial Britain* and *Coal Face* "ratifies the distinction between mental and manual labour."[18] Their assessment ignores the former film's portrayal of craft labor, as well as thirties documentary's conflicted responses to "the worker."

The craftsman's depiction as the artist of the industrial North presents further evidence of *English Journey's* and *Industrial Britain's* more permeable boundary between self and other. Both establish textual coalitions in which documentary producer and represented worker assert their craft in the face of mass production. Inverting Morris's earlier figuration of the artist as worker (in which Morris, D. G. Rossetti, and other friends formed a craft guild to bring artistry to labor), these thirties texts present the worker as artist. As Peter Stansky asserts, Morris's Firm reinforced class division through the perception that "if undoubted gentlemen, bohemian though some of them might be, were involved in matters of manufacture and design, then the pursuits themselves were considered to be at a somewhat higher level."[19] For Morris and his partners, the beauty of their writing and painting provided a standard for handicrafts; for Grierson and Auden, craft labor provided a model for filmmaking and writing.

English Journey and especially Industrial Britain close the distance between artist and worker by placing craftsmen within the canon of Western art. Unlike T. S. Eliot's "historical sense" in The Waste Land, which juxtaposes the working classes with the "classics" and thus separates them—consider, for example, the diction gap between the cockney woman and Shakespeare's Ophelia in the pub scene—these thirties texts join classes and classics through modernist temporal layering. Both read signs of classical Egypt into England's North Country. For example, Priestley declares, "These North Staffordshire workmen and the potters of Ancient Egypt share the same skill, and if they could meet and find a common language, no doubt they would have a lot to say to one another."[20] Industrial Britain's voice-over, written by Grierson, proclaims that even the glass crafter's furnace stoker performs "work as old as the Pyramids." Instead of representing a decline from past grandeur like Eliot's working classes or the Victorian craftsman, documentary's craft worker embodies a noble, living tradition.

Such allusions to the canon of decorative and high art validate not only the craftsman's work but also the documentarist's—a motivation evident especially in Industrial Britain. More allusive than Priestley's book, the film reflects the modernist influence that Ian Aitken has noted in Grierson's earlier film, Drifters. Whereas Drifters' primary modernist technique was montage editing, Industrial Britain's is the sonic temporal layering we hear in the intertexts of the narration and the music. Just before Tim Huckleby is introduced, for example, the commentator contends that if modern goblet makers donned "old Italian costumes," they "might be Venetian glass masters of the sixteenth century." Beethoven's Coriolan imparts a musical rhythm to the film's images of glass craftsmen at work, and it inflects Industrial Britain's entire glassmaking sequence with the canonical status of Romantic music. Coriolan also layers the sequence with other historical periods through its allusions to Shakespeare's play and to Roman history. Densely coded, this music does more than highlight the film's lyricism—a purpose Aitken sees in Grierson's choice of Romantic music for Drifters. Beethoven's textual presence in Industrial Britain confers "high art" status on both industrial and documentary production.[21]

The film's allusions to romantic and classical art also reveal the problematics of such temporal layering: the craftsman becomes a figure who is both timeless and timely. While the former quality elevates the craft worker, it also releases him from his historical moment and thus erases the threats posed by Britain's depression. *Industrial Britain's* narration never directly acknowledges the diminishing status of craft labor, although its insistence on "only the individual" assumes an opposing system of labor. Yet Grierson was aware of the discrepancy between the noble workmen his Film Units portrayed on the screen and the appalling conditions they often faced on the job. In his essay on the American documentary filmmaker Robert Flaherty, who codirected *Industrial Britain,* Grierson acknowledged the problem of presenting a heroic image of workers during a time of economic crisis: "It is, I know only too well, difficult to be sure of one's attitudes in a decade like this. Can we heroicize our men when we know them to be exploited? Can we romanticize our industrial scene when we know that our men work brutally and starve ignobly in it? Can we praise it—and in art there must be praise—when the most blatant fact of our time is the bankruptcy of our national management?"[22] Ultimately, Grierson's agenda followed documentary's tendency to substitute iconographic for economic power—a strategy he believed necessary to counteract narrative fictional cinema's inadequate portrayal of workers. So the widespread unemployment among England's craftsmen remains outside the conscious boundaries of *Industrial Britain;* in contrast, *English Journey* implores readers to mitigate the growing problem of foreign competition by purchasing Potteries products.

Both texts' construction of the craftsman as surrogate artist figure produces formal incongruities that momentarily disrupt the documentary frame. In *English Journey* this doubleness pressures the initial framing of the Potteries chapter. Here Priestley establishes the Potteries as both the site of fine craftsmanship and the birthplace of Arnold Bennett, whose novels had given the industrial district's "Five Towns" a literary existence. The latter triggers a textual outburst when Priestley discovers the Potteries citizens' apparent ignorance of

Bennett's work: "I wonder if there is a country in Europe in which musicians, painters, authors, philosophers, scientists, count for less than they do in this country. . . . I think it is the result of our general lack of intellectual curiosity and zest for art."[23] The sheer defensiveness of this tangential denunciation—and its abrupt ending—mark Priestley's concern about literary as well as industrial markets. In *Industrial Britain,* the doubleness of the craftsman figure brings the film's central sequence to a self-reflexive ending. Summing up modern applications of the glass industry, the narrator points out that craftsmen create lenses "for the camera that made this picture, for the projector that is showing it on the screen here." Breaking momentarily the seamless authority with which documentary usually cloaks itself, this comment highlights the constructed nature of nonfictional cinema. Thus the craftsman-artist in *English Journey* and *Industrial Britain*—as well as his counterparts in Auden's writings—fused with the documentary artist who represented him.

Grierson and Auden, in fact, invoked the craftsman in their respective models of the filmmaking and writing process. As Annette Kuhn has written, Grierson's Film Units adhered to a "'craft' model of production" that "foreground[s] the notion of talent, genius, or individual creativity." In other words, the idea of craft labor was built into the very structure of the British documentary film movement, making Grierson's team of filmmakers analogous to a craft guild. Grierson's essay on Flaherty links his filmmakers' "formidable equipment as craftsmen" to the quality behind British durable goods; Rotha's *Documentary Film* asserts that the new art form is noteworthy not only for its "social analysis" but also for its "often brilliant craftsmanship." By contrast, Grierson railed against the commercial cinema's studio production system, which he saw as filmmaking's equivalent of industrial mass production. His essays often criticized the "salesmen" and "showmen" of the studios, who were "driven by economics into artifice," because, in Kuhn's words, Grierson held "a conviction that to work in the industry is to suffer an inhibition of artistic freedom and to have one's integrity curbed according to box-office requirements." Like industrial craftsmen, the E.M.B. and G.P.O. Film Units occupied a marginal position in their industry; commercial cinema had far greater resources and distribution. As

Paul Swann points out, the E.M.B. Film Unit's budget prohibited access to sound equipment until 1932—a lack that prevented distribution to theaters.[24] Thus craft worker and documentarist felt the common threat of a mass society that devalued individual making, whether it was a Wedgwood vase, a documentary film, or a literary work.

In Auden's critical essays, the craftsman would become an even more important figure than he was for Grierson. Auden's defense of the human desire "to *make* things" in "How to Be Masters of the Machine" taps into the rich meanings that word has in the history of English poetry. As Sir Philip Sidney's 1595 treatise "The Defense of Poesy" points out, the words "poet" and "to make" are linked through Greek etymology: "We Englishmen have met with the Greeks in calling him [the poet] 'a maker.'" Through their unmatched skill, Sidney argues, poets prove that "in the most excellent work is the most excellent workman." Auden's 1935 essay "Psychology and Art To-day" considers the competing constructions of "the poet as the Possessed and as the Maker," invoking Morris to assert that "poets themselves, painfully aware of the labour involved, on the whole have inclined towards the second." At the close of the decade, W. B. Yeats's "Under Ben Bulben" would use the poet-maker figure to instruct his peers:

> Irish poets, learn your trade,
> Sing whatever is well made,
> Scorn the sort now growing up
> All out of shape from toe to top . . .

Like Auden and Morris, Yeats decried shoddy workmanship in writing—literature's equivalent of the modern factory product.[25]

In the 1930s, Mass-Observation's "Oxford Collective Poem" offered one of the boldest attempts to fashion poetry along the lines of mass production. Published in the 1937 volume of *New Verse*—the same magazine that featured Auden's poetry—this group-assembled poem derived its lines from twelve undergraduates' drafts; the final product rejected "individual" images for ones that had appeared in several participants' logs of each day's "dominant image." Besides explaining this mass writing process, Charles Madge's introduction to the "Oxford Collective Poem" also envisioned a radical reworking of poetic production. Rejecting the individualist poem that "can only be written once, under an exceptional stimulus . . . by an exceptional person," Madge hailed a vision of poet-operatives tending a writing machine: "There is nothing to prevent this kind of collective poetry from being *turned out continuously*—like daily journalism it is a *nonstop* record of events." That Madge was a poet as well as a cofounder of Mass-Observation must have troubled a craft-based poet like Auden, who would later urge the parents of would-be poets to get their children "at an early age into some Craft Trades Union."[26] Although Mass-Observation's poetry project did not flourish as did Grierson's nemesis the commercial cinema, both embraced the kind of factory-style production that threatened the decade's craft laborers.

The industrial craftsman and the documentary artist faced a fundamental shift in how things were being made. Threatened by the depression and by mass production, the thirties craftsman could hardly represent the status quo. In "How to Be Masters of the Machine," Auden points out that it was easy to "imagine yourself in the near future a worker in some gigantic factory . . . screw[ing] one nut on to each of a succession of chassis moving along a belt."[27] Such visions of mass culture prompted idealized images of craft workers as momentary stays against the encroaching factory. As we have seen, documentary's craftsman figure closed the distance between observer and observed by stressing the common work of individual artistry.

Gender freighted constructions of coal miners more heavily than it did images of craftsmen, yet documentarists' anxieties about masculinity did play a role in shaping portrayals of craft labor. For Auden and for Priestley, factory labor was not only anonymous but unmanly. "How to Be Masters of the Machine" asserts that "most of the operations in a mass production plant are of such slight importance in themselves that no one could possibly feel that doing them *made him a man*." Echoing Ruskin's earlier pronouncement that England's industrial towns "manufacture everything . . . except men," Auden concurs with his Victorian predecessor that degrading labor diminishes the worker's masculinity.[28] Yet unlike Ruskin's laborers (which included craftsmen), documentary's craftsman proved more manly than his bourgeois observers.

English Journey emphasizes this discrepancy in the scene where Priestley tries his hand at throwing and decorating pottery. Just as

Orwell's account of his descent into coal mines prompts a male gendering of his reader, so does Priestley's account of observing Wedgwood potters working their clay: "Never have I seen another substance that set up such an itch in the hand. All *your* manhood—or boyhood—ached to be at it. The lovely stuff simply asked for trouble." When Priestley attempts to make a vase, his narrative drops the heterosexual framework of male potter and female clay to establish an all-male network of reader, writer, and craftsmen. Like Orwell, who admits in *Wigan Pier* that "no conceivable amount of effort or training" could help him survive the physical toil of mining, Priestley discovers that he is physically incapable of performing the labor he observes. His comic efforts to don workmen's overalls and "grappl[e] manfully with the clay" make him a ridiculous figure in the craftsmen's eyes; the men and the "grinning lads" "roared with laughter." Priestley concludes that unlike William de Morgan, a potter who later became a novelist, he himself would prove unable to make the opposite transition because of no "confidence in my thumbs."[29] This episode from *English Journey* serves as yet another example of how images of craftsmen pressure the mind/body dualism that typically privileges the documentarist over the workers he observes. Because he lacks the worker's physical prowess, the thirties documentarist is the one who ends up being half a man.

Documenting the Coal Miner

Images of coal miners became more prominent in the middle portion of the documentary decade, and they have played a greater role in cultural memory than images of craftsmen. From the National Unemployed Workers Movement's hunger strikes of 1931–32 to the Miners' Federation stay-down strikes of 1935, from the Hardcastle family in Walter Greenwood's *Love on the Dole* to the mining communities in Orwell's *The Road to Wigan Pier*, coal miners' struggles for economic survival marked this decade of social crisis. An accompanying crisis of masculinity also shaped the coal miner in documentary representation—a factor that has not received as much critical attention. Reinforcing and undermining dominant gender constructions, the coal miner's public image reveals the sexual dynamics of documentary's male-on-male gaze; moreover, it erases the line be-

tween homosexual and heterosexual cross-class scrutiny. This instability played out not only within the images themselves, but also
within the male networks that produced them.

Because most British documentary practitioners in the 1930s were
men, and because their texts about working-class men intersected
with one another, we can see in thirties documentary film, writing,
and photography a cultural nexus of what Eve Kosofsky Sedgwick
has termed "homosocial desire." In *Between Men*, Sedgwick posits
"the potential unbrokenness of a continuum between homosocial
and homosexual" by revealing the erotic dynamics of both nonsexual
and sexual male bonds; her examples come from eighteenth- and
nineteenth-century English novels. As Sedgwick contends, the dominant culture's homophobia operates to block this continuum's visibility
for men, a disruption that bears on our own century's crisis of homo/
heterosexual definition.[30] The homosocial environment of thirties
documentary practice pressured homo/heterosexual definition most
visibly in its representations of coal miners.

When we place alongside one another images from *The Mine* (GB-
Instructional, 1935), Orwell's *Wigan Pier* (1937), and Auden's industrial love poem "I chose this lean country" (1928), the boundary between cross-class scrutiny and homoerotic looking begins to break
down. No physique proved more intriguing to the male documentarist's gaze than the coal miner's. Whereas D. H. Lawrence had fil-
tered his erotic descriptions of miners' bodies through the women
characters who watch them bathe—in *Women in Love*, for example,
Gudrun gazes at Beldover miners bathing in their backyards—thirties documentary observers preferred to bypass domestic space and
watch miners in their all-male work environments. Consider this still
from *The Mine*, an educational film shot by Frank Bundy and directed
by J. B. Holmes (fig. 3).

Fracturing the miner's body into torso and left arm, the frame's
erotic dismemberment centers on his bulging muscles. Stark frontal
lighting also contributes to this sexualized display of a man at work;
the absence of fill and backlighting shrouds the miner's head in darkness and positions the viewer as a voyeur. In *Wigan Pier*, Orwell
frames working miners with a similar gaze that gravitates toward the
torso before moving down: "It is only when you see miners down
the mine and naked that you realise what splendid men they are . . .

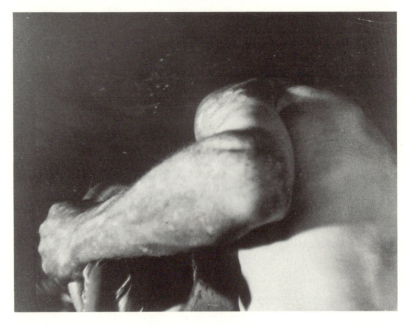

3. Still from the film *The Mine* (G. B. Instructional, Ltd., 1935). (Courtesy the Rank Organisation Plc and British Film Institute)

nearly all of them have the most noble bodies; wide shoulders tapering to slender supple waists, and small pronounced buttocks and sinewy thighs, with not an ounce of waste flesh anywhere." Orwell's verbal equivalent of the film image employs heavy sibilance to highlight the miners' individual body parts. Sharing a homoerotic as well as a cross-class gaze, *The Mine* and *Wigan Pier* illustrate the figurative dismemberments that Gregory Woods finds central to homoerotic poetry. According to Woods, male-male "sexual appraisal and activity" are analogous because "the focus of desire . . . operates obsessively in close-up"—a dynamic we also see in these documentary images of miners' bodies.[31]

Orwell's specifically *economic* appraisal also highlights the role of class difference in shaping the decade's documentary desires. For as *Wigan Pier*'s detailed account of substandard wages, household budgets, and widespread malnourishment makes clear, economic deprivation sculpted the miners' "slender" waists and lack of "waste flesh," just as strenuous manual labor sculpted their "wide shoulders" and prominent musculature. Measuring in ounces the miners' indentations and curvatures, Orwell's homoerotic economy intersects culturally not only with documentary cross-class scrutiny, but also with homosexual cross-class encounters. Bourgeois gay men's attraction to working-class men—especially younger ones—often freighted the metaphor of "going over" with homosexual meanings. The intersection of documentary's sexualized images of coal miners with Auden's industrial love poems clarifies the homosocial continuum of crossing the class frontier.

Auden set some of his most explicitly homosexual love poems in Britain's industrial regions, documentary's primary site of male identification and desire. The latent homoeroticism in "The Watershed" proves more explicit in a poem that Auden omitted from Faber's editions of *Poems,* "I chose this lean country." Consider, for example, what Woods calls the poem's "wet dream" section:

> Last night, sucked giddy down
> The funnel of my dream,
> I saw myself within
> A buried engine-room.
> Dynamos, boilers, lay
> In tickling silence, I
> Gripping an oily rail,
> Talked feverishly to one
> Who puckered mouth and brow
> In ecstasy of pain,
> "I know, I know, I know"
> And reached his hand for mine.

Here Auden's industrial North becomes more eroticized as its technological features encourage tactile experience—the machinery heightening the effect of the "tickling" atmosphere, the "oily rail" heightening the speaker's awareness of his grip. More significant is the speaker's underground male companion with his sensual "puckered mouth." Before joining this man in the "buried engine-room," the speaker traversed "this lean country" alone, examining a deserted mine and climbing "a crooked valley"; Edward Mendelson has noted Auden's use of the word *crooked* to signify homosexuality. In "The chimneys are smoking," published in the 1933 anthology *New Country* and in Auden's 1936 volume *Look Stranger!* mines become a trope for the buried, "crooked" love that must "hide underground"; Auden's speaker links himself and his male lover with "the colliers" in a world of "double-shadow."[32] From these industrial, underground enclosures (the engine room, mines), Auden creates erotic spaces safely removed from the hostile eyes that threaten homosexual lovers in early poems such as "That night when joy began." The shared terrain of Auden's industrial love poems and Orwell's erotic observations provides an important context for the British documentary film movement that Auden would join in 1935.

Grierson's mostly male film units at the Empire Marketing Board and General Post Office were perhaps the most cohesive homosocial group in which documentary practice developed in the thirties. Although men also headed the documentary collective Mass-Observation, its cross-class scrutiny of the North sometimes focused on working-class women; moreover, many volunteer Observers were women— especially during the war years. By contrast, the working environment at the E.M.B. Film Unit was, as Barnouw recounts, "strangely monastic" despite its three women employees:" Working hours were limitless. Staff members got the impression that marriage was taboo, and the existence of girl-friends was kept from Grierson. Grierson himself fell for Margaret Taylor, sister of staff member John Taylor, and they got married, but Grierson did not mention it for eighteen months. She went to work at the unit, but they never arrived or left together. . . . Grierson and his staff spent hours at the pub together, drinking and talking." Several members of this network went on to shape other documentary groups such as GB-Instructional and Strand Films. A quick glance at the all-male portrait gallery of filmmakers in Rotha's *Documentary Diary* reinforces the importance of *institutional* male-male bonds to the British documentary film movement, an important homosocial category that Sedgwick points to in *Between Men*.[33]

Like the Victorian men's settlement movement that Seth Koven has discussed, the documentary film movement brought together communities of public school and university men to observe the working classes. While the settlers departed from documentary filmmakers by establishing long-term residence in London's slums and devoting their attention to instructing boys—both groups' public activities promoted the expression of homoerotic desire. Koven's speculation about the homosexually inclined settlers might well apply to some of the documentarists: "While ostensibly these men came to heal the wounds of a class-divided nation, it seems probable that many were also driven by the need to come to terms with their own sexualities."[34] In the case of the British documentary film movement, homosexual *and* heterosexual men who scrutinized muscular coal miners also confronted their own masculinities.

I find it significant that two gay men, Auden and composer Benjamin Britten, played a key role in shaping thirties documentary film practice. Collaborating for the first time on the chorus and music to *Coal Face,* Auden and Britten drew wide acclaim for their innovative integration of verse commentary and music in the most famous G.P.O. production, *Night Mail.* They also collaborated with *The Mine's* director J. B. Holmes on a production for Strand Films.[35] Acknowledging these men's sexual orientation in the context of their film work helps to broaden our understanding of documentary's masculinity. The fact that homoerotic images of coal miners predate Auden and Britten's employment with the film movement—along with the collaborative nature of film production—renders problematic accounts of the decade that segregate gay men from their peer artists, such as Valentine Cunningham's *British Writers of the Thirties.* Cunningham pronounces that "much of the period's writing about the proletariat is vitiated by the bourgeois bugger's *specialist* regard."[36] This misguided attempt to contain the homosexual's cross-class gaze ignores not only Orwell's frank appraisal of miners' physiques, but also the documentary film movement's homoerotic voyeurism.

Jeffrey Weeks has noted that affluent British men's "fascination with crossing the class divide"—a "clearly observable" trend by the late nineteenth century—reveals "a direct continuity between male heterosexual *mores* and homosexual." To stress this continuity in thirties culture, I have used the term "homoerotic" to characterize documentary images because, as Woods contends, homoeroticism constitutes "a major, self-referential part of male sexuality as a whole." This term also suits my purposes because, like the term "documentary," it is inclusive in theory but male centered in practice. For example, Allen Ellenzweig defines the homoerotic as "feelings of desire, intimacy, admiration, or affection between members of the same sex," yet he includes only images of men in *The Homoerotic*

Photograph.[37] Similarly, thirties documentary film positions itself as championing "real" people but privileges "real men" for visual attention. If we return homoeroticism to the center of documentary practice—our century's principal discourse of reality—we can formulate new interpretations of thirties culture along the axis of gender.

Documentary's most sustained homoerotic looking at coal miners occurred within the British documentary film movement. Two productions sexualize these workers whose labor required great muscular strength and dexterity—the E.M.B. Film Unit's *Industrial Britain,* begun in 1931 and released in 1933, and the G.P.O. Film Unit's *Coal Face,* produced and released in 1935. The latter film grants more screen time to underground work scenes, thus attesting to the coal miner's increasing iconographic power during the middle of the decade. Although they had different directors, *Industrial Britain* and *Coal Face* employ remarkably similar depictions of miners' bodies; the films even share bits of the same footage. Some critics have pointed out both films' male centeredness—Colls and Dodd even note that *Coal Face*'s "only sustained close-ups are of semi-naked miners"—but they have largely ignored the homoerotic dynamics of their male-on-male gaze.[38]

In each film, an abrupt cut from shadowed groups of miners entering the shaft to a single miner removing his shirt marks a transition to more homoerotic images (fig. 4).

Because of the mine's heat and darkness, such representations might draw little comment were it not for the distinct cinematic style with which the filmmakers frame these workers. Three distinctive characteristics in these transitional shots play out in subsequent images of the miner's half-naked, bent body: brighter lighting makes the exposed flesh of the torso glisten; closer framing effects a figurative dismemberment of the miner's body; and camera angles position the viewer as a voyeur. In *Industrial Britain,* for example, the miners' muscular torsos are brightly lit while faces and heads are usually shadowed—a radical departure from the film's framing of craftsmen. The camera moves closer to miners in *Coal Face,* allowing the light to sculpt flesh contours and render sweat and body hair visible. This camera position also enables *Coal Face*'s further fragmentation of miners' bodies; while torso shots appear in both films, *Coal Face* also includes shots of miners' legs. Again, this cinematic style departs

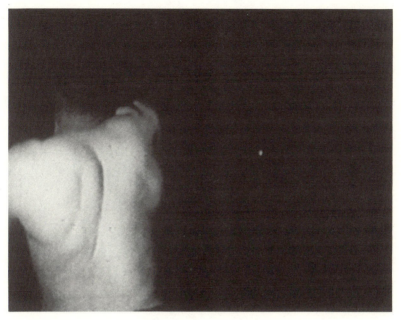

4. Coal miner at work from *Industrial Britain*. (Courtesy Kino Video)

from the documentary movement's earlier images of craftsmen; the close-up of Tim Huckleby's face is a worker's portrait rather than an erotic dismemberment. *Coal Face*'s fractured framing reflects not only what Miles and Smith call the film's "aggressively modernist" form, but also its homoerotic display of the *miner's* form. As Beatrix Campbell observes in *Wigan Pier Revisited*, "The miner's body is loved in the literature of men because of its work and because it works"; in other words, the miner's body performs both physical and cultural work as the primary site of documentary desire.[39]

Significantly, *Industrial Britain* and *Coal Face* position their viewers as voyeurs. Lighting contributes to this effect, but camera angle is most crucial here—often miners' backs are to the viewer, or their heads are turned away in profile shots. In an unusual framing from *Coal Face*, for example, the camera looks over a miner's shoulder (medium close-up) as he lifts his bottle toward his mouth and toward the viewer. This miner appears in the lower left portion of the frame, so that the surrounding darkness adds to the image's voyeuristic effect. Documentary's supposedly unobtrusive camera style takes

5. Coal miners at rest from *Coal Face* (G.P.O. Film Unit, 1935). (Courtesy the Post Office Film & Video)

on new meaning in such images; while it seemingly allows the miners to appear working and eating "naturally," it also frames them with a homoerotic gaze. The miners almost seem conscious of their erotic objectification in *Coal Face* when we see two seated men eating sandwiches (fig. 5).

Unlike other shots in which miners' glistening torsos and body hair are visible, these men face the camera *and* they have draped their shirts over their left shoulders. Acknowledging the cameraman's and viewer's gaze, these miners momentarily disrupt the film's dominant framing of workers as objects of desire. The mining sequences of *Coal Face* and *Industrial Britain* close with shots of a miner pushing a tub of coal into a dark tunnel, away from the viewer. His body's bent position displays shoulder and back muscles, and the rear angle reaffirms the cameraman's—and viewer's—voyeurism.

How did such frankly homoerotic images come to circulate in government-sponsored films, and how have critics come to ignore them? The answer lies largely in our viewing habits. Conditioned to anchor photographic images with their accompanying verbal texts, and conditioned to read films like *Industrial Britain* and *Coal Face* as rhetorical cinema, we usually grant primacy to the voice-over narrator's exposition. For example, Nichols maintains that "direct-address commentary in the British documentary of the 1930s" derives from classical rhetoric, so that "each sequence sets in place a block of argumentation that the image track illustrates." The tendency to read E.M.B. and G.P.O. films as articulating Grierson's social agenda in tandem with his essays also prompts commentary-centered readings. As a consequence of such conventions, we have learned to view the miners in these films only as socioeconomic information. *Industrial Britain* especially invites such readings because its voice-over often beckons our attention away from the images' homoeroticism—emphasizing the miners' "narrow and confined" work spaces, their "primitive method of hewing coal," the number of miners in Britain, and "the human factor" that remains in "this machine age." *Coal Face*'s commentary sometimes ventures close to acknowledging the homoerotic spectacle of miners at work; for example, while we see the miner who removed his shirt bending over, the male commentator points out that the temperature in the mine can reach eighty degrees. When we return to this shirtless miner a few shots later, the commentator explains that a miner "can work with a naked flame."[40] These references to heat and "nakedness" heighten attention to the displayed body, momentarily diverting our attention from the ongoing commentary on working conditions. In fact the innovative, polyvocal sound track of *Coal Face* offers us a good opportunity to break some of our documentary viewing habits.

With a sound track as fractured as many of its images, *Coal Face* interrupts the dominant voice-over narration with a men's spoken chorus and a women's sung chorus, as well as with Britten's discordant music. The first chorus "speaks for" the workers in the mining sequence with a litany of job titles (such as "barrowman" and "hewer"), while the second is a love poem by Auden. Of these two choruses, it is actually the *women's* that best serves my purpose of reading *Coal Face* as a homoerotic text—a dynamic that becomes clearer if we return once more to Sedgwick's *Between Men*. Her assessment of women's status in male homosocial exchange borrows from René Girard's study of how "erotic triangles" shape "the male-centered novelistic tradition of European high culture." Of particular interest to Sedgwick is the bond between rival males who form "the two active members of an erotic triangle," the passive member being a woman.[41] This schema also proves useful in assessing the status of the women's chorus in a male-centered documentary film, although there are some key differences. In both cases the "woman" facilitates negotiations between men, and the relationships between her and each male shape the text to a much smaller degree than does the relationship of the men to one another. In the case of Auden's chorus for *Coal Face,* however, woman figures only as a voice through which a male observer expresses documentary desire for a coal miner; the miner is active because of his vigorous labor, but passive because the documentary observer controls his image on the screen. We can also read this ventriloquism as a drag performance in which a gay man publicly expresses—and masks—his homosexual desires.

Neither film nor literary critics have addressed "O lurcher loving collier's" significance to *Coal Face,* much less its subversion of male gender roles. While Colls and Dodd, as well as Miles and Smith, ignore Auden's love poem in their analyses of the film, Mendelson and Lucy McDiarmid comment chiefly on its formal properties. The poem certainly proves a richer text when we return it to the contexts of the film for which it was written and the homosocial environment in which it was produced. Unlike the men's chorus that appears intermittently in *Coal Face's* second sequence, Auden's poem dominates the verbal sound track in the third sequence—even though women's bodies do not appear in this film. The women's chorus begins as the miners leave the pithead, so that the men remain objects of desire after their work is performed:

> O lurcher loving collier black as night,
> Follow your love across the smokeless hill.
> Your lamp is out and all your cages still.
> Course for her heart and do not miss
> And Kate fly not so fast,
> For Sunday soon is past,
> And Monday comes when none may kiss.
> Be marble to his soot and to his black be white.

Initially, Auden's poem seems to close off a homoerotic reading with its strict gender and color oppositions of collier/Kate, his/her, and black/white—a dichotomy that Lawrence used to heighten sexual tension between miners and women. For example, the young wife in "A Sick Collier" is "startled" when her husband returns from the pit "with a face indescribably *black* and streaked," a stark contrast to her "*white* blouse, "*white* apron" and "*fair*" complexion.[42] Yet Auden's use of such oppositions—and other formal patterns—actually points to the poem's homosocial dynamics.

When we consider the work of gender in its "elegant chiasmus and subtle rhyme scheme," this love poem hardly proves "distanced from ideological significance," as McDiarmid claims. The male/female opposition, for example, prefigures Auden's command to "Resex the pronouns" of love poems in his 1953 poem "The Truest Poetry Is the Most Feigning," a strategic alteration that Alan Sinfield reads as "a closeted gay aesthetic." Note also how the *Coal Face* poem's irregular rhyme scheme (ABBCDDCA) links the male figures of lines one and eight. More telling, the poem's series of imperatives *directs* the collier and "Kate" toward one another, suggesting that this pairing is not "natural" behavior (Kate's impulse is to "fly"). These cues for the collier's and Kate's gestures anticipate Judith Butler's performative theory of gender, in which any "gender identity . . . is performatively constituted by the very 'expressions' that are said to be its results."[43] If the poem's imperative heterosexual coupling is in effect no more than a set of stage directions, then the true site of desire in *Coal Face* is the underground enclosures where male documentary observers watch half-naked miners.

While "O lurcher loving collier" positions *Coal Face's* male viewers within its homosocial network, the poem's performance by a women's chorus also creates a network of gay male viewers who could interpret Auden's poem as a drag performance. A related chorus that Auden wrote for women's voices provides fuller access to this gay coding; like the *Coal Face* poem, it expresses desire for a miner. The campy love song "Rhondda Moon," from Auden and Christopher Isherwood's play *The Dog beneath the Skin* (1936), parodies the way documentary representation eroticized worker's bodies; significantly, the play debuted one month before Auden left the G.P.O. Film Unit. At the same time, "Rhondda Moon" appropriates documentary's socially acceptable form of homoeroticism to represent homosexuality. The song occurs when a chorus joins Madame Bubbi—"an immense woman in sequin dress"—on the Nineveh Hotel's cabaret stage:

On the Rhondda
My time I squander
Watching for my miner boy:
He may be rough and tough
But he surely is hot stuff
And he's slender, to-me-tender,
He's my only joy:
Lovers' meeting,
Lovers' greeting,
O his arms will be around me soon!
For I am growing fonder
Out yonder as I wander
And I ponder 'neath a Rhondda moon![44]

This over-the-top performance, culminating in an avalanche of feminine internal and end rhymes, intersects with documentary's discrepancies between economic and iconographic power. Auden locates the singers' object of desire in a Welsh mining district hit especially hard by the depression; the Rhondda was also the site of the Parc and Dare miners' stay-down strike. Unlike his desiring observers, the song's struggling miner has no "time" to "squander" but possesses the riches of a "rough and tough" yet "slender" body. This latter adjective recalls Orwell's economic appraisal of "slender supple waists" in *Wigan Pier*; the erotics behind both texts hinge on class difference.

Another network of key words points to explicitly homosexual meanings in "Rhondda Moon" that depend on class and *age* difference. As Koven notes, late Victorian and Edwardian culture's definitions of the word "rough" referred generally to lads (that is, boys), especially to those of the working classes. Yet "rough" also acquired sexual connotations in gay circles; for example, "rough trade" meant "working-class, usually youthful male prostitution." When we add to this cultural meaning the inside joke behind the lead singer's name—Isherwood had a young, working-class boyfriend nicknamed Bubi—we can see that "Rhondda Moon" performs the double act of sending up documentary desire while representing homosexual liaisons. Humphrey Carpenter's biography recounts Auden's introducing Isherwood to Bubi and other boys who frequented Berlin's Cosy Corner, a working-class bar. Because documentary's public images of miners shared a male-male gaze across class lines, they provide a partial screen for Auden's private network of gay references. The female singers give "Rhondda Moon" additional cover, just as they do for the song in *Coal Face;* both women's choruses about miners are, in effect, drag performances—Madame Bubbi's size and costume certainly suggest a drag queen. In the homosocial environment that shaped the coal miner's image, Auden's dubbing in of women's voices intersects with documentary's socioeconomic framing to allow the expression of homoerotic desire. Thus documentary practice proves to be another way of knowing that was, in Sedgwick's words, "structured—indeed, fractured" by our century's "endemic crisis of homo/heterosexual definition."[45]

In most examinations of the 1930s, critics have focused on class alone as the driving force behind the decade's social instability—and thus as the driving force behind both Auden's poetry and documentary representation. But another factor proved equally important in negotiating the decade's uncertainties and establishing documentary—the social act of "being a man." Documentary texts of the thirties mark a crisis of masculinity in their often contradictory assertions about manliness in the face of industrial Britain. While documentary anxieties yielded texts that subscribed to dominant constructions of masculinity—most notably the documentarist as swaggering explorer of working-class terrain—these same anxieties also generated texts that challenged traditional masculinity.

Too young to have "proved" their manhood in the Great War and as yet untested by Spain and World War II, the "documentary men" of the thirties found their gender role to be a less scripted performance than did their fathers and older brothers. As Isherwood expressed it in *Lions and Shadows,* the culture's determining "Test" of masculinity was absent: "Like most of my generation, I was obsessed by a complex of terrors and longings connected with the idea of 'War.' 'War,' in this purely neurotic sense, meant The Test. The test of your courage, of your maturity, of your sexual prowess: 'Are you really a Man?' Subconsciously, I believe, I longed to be subjected to this test; but I also dreaded failure." Yet for the Auden generation, one group of men did not need a war to prove their masculinity, for they were, as Priestley put it, "continually and severely tested" in industrial Britain's coal mines.[46] The "buried" sites of coal mining *and* of homoerotic desire are exposed in Auden's poems of the thirties,

Orwell's *Wigan Pier,* and the documentary films *Industrial Britain* and *Coal Face.* Reclaimed as a homoerotic site, documentary representation presents alternative masculinities that challenge standard accounts of the thirties.

Night Mail and Britain's Industrial Unconscious

As we have seen, industrial Britain generated contradictions in documentary texts of the 1930s, sometimes unsettling dominant formulations of workers and masculinity. This context is crucial to understanding *Night Mail,* the British documentary film movement's most famous production. The film depicts a postal train's nightly run from London to Glasgow and remains noteworthy for its creative use of sound (the credits list Alberto Cavalcanti, Britten, and Auden under "Sound Direction"). Typically, discussions of *Night Mail* focus either on its rhythmic integration of Auden's poem with the editing and music (Barnouw, Aitken) or on its depiction of postal workers (Richard Barsam, Miles and Smith). Departing from previous critics, I will focus on the metaphoric black country through which the train travels.

Night Mail, released in 1936, marks the turning point of the documentary film movement's relationship to industrial Britain, as well as the point where cultural memory begins to repress this riddlesome region. By the time the documentary decade came to a close, the G.P.O. Film Unit would embrace national consensus building to support the British war effort. In 1939 the unit was transferred to the Ministry of Information (the same year that Mass-Observation vacated its northern headquarters to focus on home front reportage); anticipating this documentary shift, industrial Britain would begin to disappear from representation with *Night Mail.*[47] The film participates in forming an *industrial unconscious* of Britain's "other" country by depicting a labor performed while most of Britain sleeps.

Although the train's northward journey seems to intersect with the thirties phenomenon that Orwell called "a curious cult of Northernness,"[48] *Night Mail* represses industrial images of muscular workers and smoking chimneys. Instead, its dominant version of "the worker" is the postal employee—efficient, jovial, and fully clothed. Yet a trace of the homoeroticism of *Industrial Britain* and *Coal Face* appears

6. Railway workers from *Night Mail* (G.P.O. Film Unit, 1936). (Courtesy the Post Office Film & Video)

briefly in *Night Mail's* opening sequence. As the postal train approaches a railway yard, we see a group of men working on the track (the low lighting and the sound of pickaxes evoke mining scenes from *Industrial Britain* and *Coal Face*). These workers step aside as the train—the primary subject of the film—rushes past. Instead of following the "postal special," however, the next shot disconnects itself from the narration to linger a moment on railyard workers' bodies (fig. 6).

Framed in darkness, this unanchored image from *Night Mail's* industrial unconscious shows two workmen whose rolled-up sleeves reveal their left biceps. The man on the left rests his arm against his pickax handle, his cap shadowing his eyes, while the man on the right lifts both forearms to light a pipe—a gesture that diverts this worker's eyes from the camera and causes his biceps to flex. An abrupt cut to the rushing train ends the sequence's homoerotic reverie. From this point onward, the camera gravitates toward the jacketed postal workers who perform their tasks under fuller light. (*Night Mail's* "on-board" mail sorting scenes were filmed in a studio.) Work remains a male activity in *Night Mail;* its two women are relegated to the domestic space behind the counter at a station coffee shop. But homoerotic images of workers' bodies no longer drive documentary desire—a sign that the rugged, masculine "North" has lost some of its potency.

Smoking chimneys—documentary's stock image of the black countries—are also curiously marginal in this northward-journeying film. Industrial Britain's first conscious appearance in *Night Mail* occurs in the third sequence, which begins after the postal train has left Crewe station. Depicting the on-board sorting, bagging, and delivery of mail, this sequence opens by bringing the industrial North into its framing commentary: "North—with one hundred tons of new letters to sort. The postal special picks up and distributes the mail of industrial England. The mines of Wigan—the steel works of Warrington— the machine shops of Preston." Although the commentator's enumeration of industrial towns could have invited a trio of representative images—after all, the G.P.O. Film Unit had appropriate stock footage of darkened mines, steel mills, and machinery—only a single tracking shot out the train window brings industry into the frame. This shot of a smokeless chimney and a platform resembling a pithead comes between the second and third sentences quoted above.[49] When Wigan is named, we see high-tension wires; when the other towns are named, we see a darkened screen. A cut to a black screen punctuated by the ghostly procession of train lights ends this flow of images and, more significantly, relegates the chimney shot to the film's industrial unconscious. From this repressed textual space, images of Britain's metaphoric black country will return in the final sequence to momentarily unsettle *Night Mail's* conscious promotion of the British civil service.

Appropriately, the thirties poet most associated with the industrial North provided the verse commentary that supplants *Night Mail's* dominant commentary in the final sequence. Auden's poem anchors this portion of the film, which depicts the postal train crossing the Cheviot Hills into Scotland. The original "Night Mail" poem opened with these lines: "North, north, north / To the country of the Clyde

and the Firth of Forth."[50] Although the film version cut this direct invocation of the North, it nonetheless lingers in the altered poem if we
read its first line as a pun: "This is the night mail crossing the border." Just as the postal train has crossed the Scottish border, *Night
Mail* itself has crossed borders metaphorically by leaving the scene of
Britain's "other" country that had drawn the documentary film movement's gaze in the early thirties. As the poem continues, it triggers
two afterimages of smoking chimneys—brief and sporadic ripples in
Night Mail's dominant flow of images.

These unpredictable returns disrupt relations between text and
image so that Auden's poem becomes a metaphoric commentary on
the film's repression of black country scenes. Drawing attention to
Night Mail's pastoral vision of Britain, the poem comments metatex-
tually on this image that documentary had previously rejected. The
final sequence opens with a fade-in to a pan across grassy hills—a
shot that establishes the film's dominant landscape as a rural one and
segues to long shots of the train crossing the Cheviots. But when the
sequence reaches the poem's third stanza (one of the slower-paced
stanzas that Grierson reads), the verbal text begins to clash with the
flow of images by invoking an industrial landscape:

> Dawn freshens, the climb is done.
> Down towards Glasgow she descends
> Toward the steam tugs, yelping down the glade of cranes
> Towards the fields of apparatus, the furnaces
> Set on the dark plain like gigantic chessmen.
> All Scotland waits for her;
> In the dark glens, beside the pale-green sea lochs
> Men long for news.

Initially cooperating with *Night Mail's* pastoralism, the stanza pressures the film's separation of rural from industrial scenes in its central lines. Auden's double landscape—"*glade* of cranes," "*field* of apparatus"—evokes the blending of nature and machinery in shots
from *Industrial Britain* and *Coal Face*. But *Night Mail's* editing allows
only one industrial shot, a smoking chimney that appears briefly
after the word "apparatus." Visually contained within shots of grassy
hillsides, the metaphoric black country's return in this segment hinges

on Auden's verbal images. But it will return once more at the end of the fourth stanza, this time departing from the verbal text entirely. Stuart Legg reads this rapid-paced portion of the poem, which catalogs various types of mail:

> The chatty, the catty, the boring, adoring,
> The cold and official and the heart's outpouring,
> Clever, stupid, short and long,
> The typed and the printed and the spelt all wrong.[51]

A shot of two large, smoking chimneys appears just before we hear the final line of Auden's litany of letters. Unlike the sequence's first chimney shot that was dissolved in and out, this more jarring entry of black country imagery is cut in from a shot of the train's engine. Here industrial Britain returns to unsettle *Night Mail*'s controlling commentary, only to be dissolved to a long shot of a city (presumably Glasgow) that sets up the poem's oddly dormant final stanza.

In this segment of *Night Mail*'s closing sequence, the postal train completes its journey to Glasgow—and its metaphorical journey of repression and return. Auden's final stanza, which Grierson reads, emphasizes the theme of sleep:

> Thousands are still asleep
> Dreaming of terrifying monsters
> Or a friendly tea beside the band at Cranston's or Crawford's;
> Asleep in working Glasgow, asleep in well-set Edinburgh,
> Asleep in granite Aberdeen.
> They continue their dreams
> But shall wake soon and long for letters.

As Miles and Smith assert, the postal employees perform their vital labor for Britain "while that community sleeps on in blissful ignorance."[52] Yet this is not the only ignorance—or irony—in the verse commentary. For *Night Mail* itself seems unaware of the industrial terrain it has traveled through, its textual journey literally bypassing the scene that had once compelled documentary scrutiny. Unlike the three industrial towns named earlier in the film, each Scottish city is paired with an illustrative image (a giant crane for Glasgow, a castle wall for Edinburgh, and a harbor for Aberdeen). The spoken text has reasserted control over the flow of images so that industrial Britain hovers outside the documentary frame, like a dormant image from a dream. Technically, the use of dissolves and stationary framing gave the sequence's earlier chimney shots the hazy appearance of dream sequences in narrative fictional cinema. Depopulated of the industrial workers that had animated previous documentary films, *Night Mail*'s images of black countries now "sleep" in cultural memory. As the "terrifying" dreams in the *Night Mail* poem and the unpredictable industrial shots suggest, however, industrial Britain's sleep can be an uneasy one.

Auden and Documentary Film in the 1990s

By asking how workers disrupt the documentary frame as well as the standard question of how documentary frames workers, this chapter has shown that thirties documentary practice both unsettled *and* reinforced dominant social constructions when it scrutinized the working classes. To these questions I now add a third: How does this unstable worker challenge our contemporary assumptions about Auden, documentary, and the thirties? In other words, How might my examination of craftsmen and coal miners revise literary and film criticism in the 1990s?

Ever since Auden emigrated to America in 1939, critics have divided his career into two parts: early (English) and late (American). Once in place, this governing opposition began to accrue additional meanings that define the competing halves in terms of commitment. Stan Smith offers a deliberately reductive summary of this "moral fable." In one version, an angry young man wisely abandons Freud and Marx when he sees the atrocities in Spain, converts to Christianity, and becomes "a grand old man of letters." In the other, a politically committed poet falls from grace, turns his back on war-torn Europe, and "proclaim[s] his reconciliation with the status quo."[53] Both fables claim that Auden's social engagement ended with the thirties; they disagree over whether his "true voice" was conservative or progressive. From this master plot have derived other oppositions that work to disengage Auden's career from the socioeconomic concerns he addressed in the 1930s: the separation of politics and art, and the separation of public and private domains. These are, ironically, the very dividing lines that would not hold in many thirties texts—including Auden's poems and documentary films. But according to the master plot, "early" Auden was political and public, while "late" Auden was aesthetic and private.

The politics/art division often pits ethical and aesthetic agendas against one another in Auden criticism by assuming that the two are never really joined except through the artist's often misguided efforts. In Frederick Buell's *W. H. Auden as a Social Poet* (1973), for example, socially engaged art becomes "a major dilemma for the artist-fellow traveler who is not willing to *sacrifice* his art altogether to politics" yet must "*commit* himself by *submitting* his art to a political theme and perhaps even use." In other words, "politics" will overpower "art" when the two cohabit a text. This forced competition takes place not only in assessments of individual texts, but also in assessments of Auden's career. A recent example is Lucy McDiarmid's *Auden's Apologies for Poetry* (1990), which enriches our understanding of the later career by proposing a "New York" Auden who "devoted his imaginative energies to commentary on art." In her version of the early/late master plot, the New York Auden set out to undermine art "with greater consistency than he had ever used to undermine 'bourgeois' society."[54] Because the class issue becomes *the* political subject of the thirties—both in Auden criticism and in film criticism—McDiarmid is in effect invoking the "politics/art" opposition in her division of early and late Auden's poetic subjects. In other words, the shift to art indicates that Auden is no longer concerned with class and thus no longer the engaged poet of the thirties.

But as we have seen, Auden's thirties essays addressed both class *and* art by linking craft workers and artists, and this link anticipates the work of the "New York" Auden who addressed the art of writing in *The Dyer's Hand*. "The Poet and the City" (1962), which McDiarmid cites to establish her governing point about art's frivolity, elaborates on the same threatened artist-craftsman figure that Auden addressed in "How to Be Masters of the Machine" and the *I Believe* anthology. Like these earlier essays, "The Poet and the City" asserts that only the "maker" escapes the degrading nature of mass labor: "A man can be proud of being a worker—someone, that is, who fabricates enduring objects." By making the Poet this essay's central figure and calling art "gratuitous" and "frivolous," Auden in no way disengages from the socioeconomic arena of masculinity, work, and workers that animated so many of his thirties texts. Moreover, Auden's Poet *intervenes* in culture by challenging mass society's labor practices: "In our age, the mere making of a work of art is itself a political act."[55] For the later Auden, then, poetry remained an alternative labor practice in an age of mass production. Writing poetry may be a "frivolous" and "gratuitous" activity in modern culture, but it was also the way Auden earned his living. This alternative model—Auden as craft worker—pressures dividing lines that would pit art against class, poetry against politics.

Like the politics/art opposition, the forced competition between public and private experience can also limit our understanding of Auden's work. Again a myth of separate spheres puts asunder what culture joins together, this time by assuming that "private" experience can exist independent of public life. Otherwise, why would critics consider Auden's poems that challenge this dividing line so remarkable? For example, Samuel Hynes reads "A Summer Night" ("Out on the lawn I lie in bed") as one of the Auden generation's key poems because "it places the traditionally private feelings of lyric poetry in the public world of history, where politics and economics are real forces, and hunger is more urgent than love." In the poem Auden joins images of privileged lovers with images of hungry masses; the eyes into which his speaker is "glad to look" become the eyes of "gathering multitudes outside / Whose glances hunger worsens."[56] Such images show the inevitable fusion of "public" and "private," rendering problematic those interpretations that pit the terms against one another.

Gregory Woods's homoerotic reading of Auden in *Articulate Flesh* (1987) challenges the "public/private" opposition in Auden studies by bringing the poet's own life into the frame of analysis. Focusing on love poems, Woods questions critical reluctance to "grant [Auden's] sexual orientation any but the most limited relevance to his work." Most critics, he rightly argues, segregate such "private" matters from Auden's "public" work of publishing poetry. By recovering the "private," homosexual Auden, Woods begins a reconstruction of the "public" Auden that continues in the recent film *Four Weddings and a Funeral;* its funeral scene reveals the poet's sexual orientation and recites one of his love poems during a eulogy—a form of public address. Yet when Woods turns to what I call the industrial love poems of the thirties, his analysis at times reinforces the very public/private bifurcation he otherwise challenges. Characterizing Auden's "early mode," Woods writes: "Despite critical characterisation of him as a 'pylon' poet, whose world was industrial Britain, his actual landscape was that of the brain." Here Woods's restoration of the "private" Auden restricts the significance of the poet's industrial terrain to one meaning—a psychological landscape. When "private" readings seek to close off "public" ones, they operate in the same manner as the exclusionary "public" readings Woods decries. In this case, the intersection of industrial Britain's socioeconomic and sexual dynamics would broaden the revisionist implications of Woods's analysis. Thirties images of coal miners show that the Black Country *facilitated* rather than blocked the expression of homoerotic desire—both in the explicitly homosexual poems that Woods addresses and in the documentary texts this chapter examines. As Auden writes in his review of Rotha's *Documentary Film*, "the private life and the emotions are facts like any others," so a lyric poem that showed no life outside the lovers' embrace would be as limited as a documentary film that showed no life outside the mine or factory.[57]

The issue of social engagement has begun to occupy the margins of recent Auden criticism, but it has remained at the center of critical debates over the British documentary film movement. Here the governing opposition codes the documentary movement either as a progressive champion of the working classes or as a reactionary tool of the state. As Aitken points out in his introduction to *Film and Reform* (1990), the first view generated from the writings of those who worked within the documentary movement; they presented "a heroic and successful struggle by talented innovators" to further social equality with "positive representations of working-class experience." The second view rightly questions the documentarists' relationship to the workers they represented but often takes an equally extreme position. For example, in his introduction to the revisionist anthology *British Cinema: Traditions of Independence* (1980), Paul Willemen asserts that the traditional view of "Griersonism" as a progressive cinematic movement is "out of all proportion to its conservative stance." He also labels the E.M.B. and G.P.O. Film Units as tools of "a particularly reactionary state apparatus" that aimed to "integrate, use, and thus defuse" a more "oppositional" independent cinema.[58] If we restore E.M.B. and G.P.O. films' representations of workers to their full documentary context, we must rethink the critiques of the 1970s and 1980s—acknowledging both the multiplicity of thirties workers and the contradictory responses of the documentarists who depicted them. My analysis of documentary's craftsman and coal miner, respectively, complicates two of the major issues that such revisionist film criticism addresses: documentarists' relation to workers and documentarists' relation to the state.

We can see the first issue in Kuhn's contribution to *British Cinema*, which addresses Grierson's preferred craft model of collaborative production. Noting that screen credits to E.M.B. and G.P.O. productions list individual filmmakers—however unreliable these credits might be—Kuhn asserts the importance of individual authorship to this film practice. At this point her analysis intersects with my own in marking common ground between documentary filmmakers and craft labor. Yet when Kuhn factors in the production mode of "the workers' filmmaking groups" (one of the "oppositional" practices Willemen favors), their uninterrogated "collective" practice begins to operate as a progressive default setting against which to position the British documentary film movement.[59] The implication is that because of the E.M.B. and G.P.O. Film Units' collaborative form of production, they are structurally opposed to the working classes they represent—an opposition that would make the "collective" documentarist closer to "the worker." This forced competition between "collaborative" and "collective" production generates a series of binary oppositions that push each mode to opposite sides of the class line: individual/group, collaborative/collective, documentarist/worker.

But as we have seen, the craftsman was a part both of thirties labor organization *and* of documentary discourse, and this worker occupies both the "individual" and the "collaborative" side of Kuhn's dividing lines. Moreover, the instability of the term "worker" in thirties discourse should caution us against conflating groups like the Workers' Film and Photo League with the working classes. I agree with Kuhn—and with Willemen—that the dominance of Grierson's productions in film history and criticism can work against our need to find alternative documentary models from the thirties; yet some of these alternatives may lie *within* the British documentary film movement as well as outside it. Constructing the E.M.B. and G.P.O. Film Units as unitary practices denies their competing images of male workers, slowing the same recovery process that revisionists rightly seek.

A second major issue in revisionist film criticism—the documentary movement's relation to the state—also drives the progressive/reactionary debate. Kuhn, for example, asserts that the E.M.B. and G.P.O. Film Units' state sponsorship "meant that any 'social' concern could not readily inform a politically oppositional film practice." In other words, the documentary movement could not subvert the state it depended on for financial support, and any social criticism must be so oblique as to render it politically ineffective. Miles and Smith propose one way the documentary movement muted social protest in their book *Cinema, Literature and Society* (1987), asserting that "gender coding played an important role in displacing the class issue" in films such as *Drifters, Coal Face,* and *Night Mail.* They argue that in *Coal Face,* class conflict "is resolved by inflecting the issue in gender terms," so that "the class issue is overdetermined by gender." Although Miles and Smith's reading rightly foregrounds the maleness of these documentary films, its pitting of gender against class (and politics) contains several problematic assumptions. First, in assuming that documentary's "true" subject is class, and the working classes in particular, Miles and Smith actually *perpetuate* the same class line that they question in these films. Second, their analysis assumes that, as Willemen puts it, the 1930s were primarily a time of "acute economic and political crises."[60] This position ignores the accompanying crisis of masculinity—also a social crisis—that proves equally important in shaping thirties culture and documentary practice. Finally, Miles and Smith assume that by foregrounding gender, the documentary movement somehow closes down the possibility of subversion. But if they expanded their point about the films' "male world" to include sexuality and the documentarists themselves, Miles and Smith might reconsider the male-on-male gaze of *Coal Face*—and thus acknowledge the subversion of publicly screening these homoerotic images of coal miners in a state that criminalized homosexuality.

Once we stop reading thirties documentary texts as position papers on the class question, we can begin to see that their contradictions often show a confusion about the working classes on the part of culture instead of a lack of commitment on the part of the producer. Thus the vocal shifts, outrageous invectives, and vexing ambiguities of Auden's infamous poem "A Communist to Others" are not only, as Cunningham claims, signs of his "wavering social allegiances," but also signs of "the worker's" power to unsettle thirties discourse:

> Comrades who when the sirens roar
> From office shop and factory pour
>   'Neath evening sky;
> By cops directed to the fug
> Of talkie-houses for a drug
> Or down canals to find a hug
>   Until you die:[61]

When does the comrade address "others" like him? When does he address the bourgeois men as "others"? Is he the poem's only speaker? Riddled with discursive instabilities, this contribution to the *New Country* anthology of 1933 participates in documentary negotiations with working-class men. Like the split between individual craftsman and mass laborer in *Industrial Britain*'s schizophrenic construction of the British worker, the working-class "communist" of Auden's poem refuses to stay on one side of thirties culture's dividing lines.

Auden's early writings and British documentary practice intersect with one another, prompting us to reexamine "the worker" of the thirties in a fuller cultural context. As we have seen, rival representations of craftsmen and coal miners reveal this worker to be less stable than conventional criticism of the thirties allows. Clearly we must revise the "commitment" model for assessing images of workers, which assumes not only a fixed "worker" but also a stable documentary practice that responded to workers in uniform fashion.

We must also acknowledge masculinity's crucial roles in shaping thirties documentary discourse. Laura Mulvey's influential essay on the male gaze in narrative fictional cinema helped establish intersections of gender and genre in contemporary critical practice. Although work in gender studies has expanded considerably—interrogating representations of men's bodies as well as women's, invoking homosexual paradigms as well as heterosexual ones—narrative genres remain central in providing examples for literary and film critics who assess the construction of gender and sexuality. By contrast, nonfiction (especially documentary) literature and film figure largely in critical discussions of social class. When recent critics such as Nichols and Rabinowitz do bring gender into the documentary frame, they usually focus their inquiries on images of women. The verbal and visual texts I have examined here remind us that documentary discourse has offered a forum on masculinity since the genre's emergence in the thirties.

3

DOCUMENTARY AND MODERNISM

Public Collage in *Letters from Iceland*

WHAT WOULD an alternative documentary practice look like? Instead of positioning those it represents within a governing frame, documentary could acknowledge its own inevitable disruption by placing itself under scrutiny. A plural *and* self-scrutinizing documentary discourse could expose the framing narration as an "idea of order," to borrow modernist poet Wallace Stevens's phrase, and could experiment with combinations of alternative textual voices. As we saw in the previous chapter, W. H. Auden's verse commentaries for *Coal Face* and *Night Mail* reveal the productive tensions documentary can create between poetic and rhetorical discourses. By reminding us of documentary's literary contexts, these and other "cinepoems" of the 1930s offer contemporary practitioners ways of reconceiving the genre.

Films were not the decade's only prominent documentary medium; the documentary book also emerged as a new means of representing social reality. In England and especially in America, several literary figures contributed to books that combined photographs and words to address contemporary crises. For example, George Orwell examined impoverished British coal miners in *The Road to Wigan Pier* (1937), and James Agee explored destitute American tenant farmers in *Let Us Now Praise Famous Men* (1941). Archibald MacLeish's *Land of the Free* (1938), which addresses America's Dust Bowl migration, emulated thirties cinepoems by pairing lines of poetry with documentary photographs; he even labeled his poem the book's "Sound Track."

Auden's name has not entered into previous accounts of the documentary book's emergence, yet his and Louis MacNeice's *Letters from*

Iceland (1937) predates MacLeish's better-known integration of poetry, photographs, and documentary cinema. Unlike Auden's book,
Land of the Free borrows from film to create a visual unity. A bold line
underscores the "Sound Track" label on the initial page and continues across the top of every left-hand page; each contains a section of
MacLeish's poem. On every right-hand page, a single uncaptioned
photograph appears. *Letters from Iceland,* by contrast, combines poetry, prose, captions, photographs, and other visual images in a discontinuous form. Although it does not focus on a particular social
problem, this unusual book sometimes sets its local observations
against what Auden calls "the orchestral background" of growing
crises in Europe—the Nazi regime in Germany and Franco's military
buildup in Spain.[1] A fragmented text that appropriates the discourses
of poetry, rhetorical documentary, travelogue, and high modernism,
Letters from Iceland suggests strategies for breaking out of conventional documentary framings.

Auden began to search for alternative documentary forms in
1936—the year he reviewed Paul Rotha's book *Documentary Film,* left
the G.P.O. Film Unit, and traveled to Iceland with a commission to
write a travel book. Iceland had fascinated Auden since childhood
because his father traced the family name to that country and taught
the Auden boys Norse legends; Iceland also attracted him because he
embraced the mystique that thirties culture attributed to northern lo-
cales. Yet the resulting book, *Letters from Iceland,* often disrupts its
account of that country with Auden's responses to his experience
with documentary film. Through its verbal and visual interplay, this
documentary travelogue both incorporates and questions Auden's
film work, making several references to his former G.P.O. colleagues
in the process. When *Letters from Iceland* first appeared in 1937,
Auden was negotiating anew with documentary in his efforts to represent the Spanish Civil War and support the Republican side. At
the decade's close in 1939, his documentary travelogue of the Sino-
Japanese war (*Journey to a War*) would adapt the photo-textual form
of *Letters from Iceland* and the social advocacy of *Spain* in yet another
attempt to capture the political crises that would coalesce into World
War II.

This chapter focuses on Auden's contributions to *Letters from Iceland,* which constitute most of this critically neglected text. Both

Auden scholars and critics of travel writing justify their dismissal by invoking the book's lack of conventional structure; for example, A. T. Tolley's study of thirties poetry finds *Letters from Iceland* "too filled out with extraneous material," while Paul Fussell declares that its fragmented narrative (along with that of *Journey to a War*) signals "the decadent stage in the course of the between-the-wars travel book." For those Auden critics who do discuss it, *Letters from Iceland* becomes either pure entertainment (Frederick Buell calls it a "literary holiday") or a social commentary on England from abroad (Tom Paulin sees "a serious political intention" at work).[2] All these critics have two things in common: they restrict *Letters from Iceland*'s cultural domain to travel books, and they ignore the implications of its radical discontinuity.

In its fullest cultural context, *Letters from Iceland* intersects with three male-dominated forms of the twentieth century—travel literature, documentary, and high modernism. The first category has defined previous inquiries into what contemporary reviewer Edwin Muir called "a pleasantly formless book."[3] I am not discounting *Letters from Iceland*'s status as an atypical travel book, a feature that surely motivated its recent reissue in Paragon House's Armchair Traveller series. But my analysis will focus on documentary and high modernist influences to consider *Letters from Iceland* in a new light. This approach offers two advantages over standard interpretations. First, the book's connections to documentary prompt more attention to Auden's photographs, thus recovering more of the visual Auden that previous commentators have ignored. Second, the book's indebtedness to high modernism points to the purposeful disjunction Auden achieves by mixing visual and verbal media.

In granting considerable attention to Auden's photographs, my analysis invites us to expand our conception of the thirties documentary book, which we usually think of as pairing the work of a professional writer and a professional photographer. American documentary books are largely responsible for this dualistic model because they established the careers of some of our century's major photographers. Walker Evans's stark portraits of tenant farmers and Dorothea Lange's compelling depictions of migrant workers remain among our most haunting images from the thirties. By contrast, the photographs in Auden's documentary travelogues are snapshots that range from thoughtfully composed portrayals of workers and industry to humorously awkward exposures of local inhabitants and fellow tourists. He admits freely in *Letters from Iceland* that his photographs include "some out of focus, some with wrong exposures." This amateur status has prompted Jefferson Hunter to pronounce that *Letters from Iceland, Journey to a War,* and other photo-texts with authors' snapshots "make little real use of their illustrations."[4] I find the assumptions behind such judgments limiting to our understanding not only of thirties photo-textual practice, but also of photography itself.

First, not all documentary books have photographs by a single, professional photographer, yet their visual impact still plays an important role in their overall effect. For example, Valentine Cunningham points to the cage motif in *Wigan Pier's* photographs of miners' dwellings (we see several barred windows, iron rails, and grates). Although we do not know which photographers or even how many produced these images, they nonetheless present a visual style that shapes readers' responses to Orwell's verbal descriptions of poverty. The odd array of snapshots in *Letters from Iceland* drew comments from several reviewers; Edward Sackville-West concluded that "the photographs are sometimes beautiful and invariably disarming," while the *Times Literary Supplement's* reviewer pronounced them "usually good and always intelligent." Second, not all photographs aim at artistic status, yet they can nonetheless perform cultural work. As critical interest in family photography attests, amateur snapshots can both prompt emotion and reflect ideology. (For example, Judith Williamson has discussed the family photo album's convention of depicting "happy, product-consuming families.")[5] In their commentary on *Letters from Iceland,* both Buell and Paulin incorporate readings of an Auden photograph to reinforce their discussion of the book's political aspects. Now that the photographs reappear in the most recent edition of *Letters from Iceland*—unlike the most recent edition of *Wigan Pier*—we have the opportunity to further explore their impact on Auden's public collage.

Letters from Iceland certainly devotes some attention to the country and its inhabitants, but Auden's primary concern is a more fundamental one—the politics of representation. Taking into account the film work Auden had completed just before his Iceland journey, this chapter reads *Letters from Iceland* as a self-reflexive documentary by a second-generation modernist. Through his photographs and words, Auden mixes the populism he saw in thirties documentary with the fragmentation he inherited from high modernist collage. These modes often contend with one another as he seeks a less aggressive, more socially conscious gaze than either can produce alone. In *Letters from Iceland,* Auden experiments with camera framing and with collage form in order to blur the line between observer and observed. Creating images with pen and camera made him more self-conscious about representation, and he came to recognize the inherent authority behind both documentary and high modernism. The achievements and limitations of *Letters from Iceland*'s alternative form prove crucial to understanding Auden's eventual disillusionment with socially conscious art.

A brief chapter-by-chapter summary gives some indication of the book's striking discontinuity, along with the portions I will emphasize in my discussion. Most chapters are individual "letters"—in verse, prose, or both—that do not make up a continuous narration. Chapter 1 presents the first part of *Letter to Lord Byron,* a long poem that Auden divides into five separate chapters. Since this witty social commentary has received far more critical attention than any other part of *Letters from Iceland,* I will refer to *Letter to Lord Byron* only in the context of the book's relation to documentary and collage. The next chapter is addressed to Christopher Isherwood and contains Auden's poem "Journey to Iceland." MacNeice's first contribution, chapter 3, justifies the writers' decision to make their journey. The following chapter, "For Tourists," provides typical guidebook information about such matters as currency and transportation. Chapter 5 continues *Letter to Lord Byron,* followed by an unusual chapter containing quotations from various travel books on Iceland (Auden titles it "Sheaves from Sagaland"). Significant because of its public collage, "Sheaves" demonstrates the ways Auden revises high modernism to create a double exposure of Icelanders and foreign observers. In chapter 7, "Letter to R. H. S. Crossman," Auden explores the concept of framing by pitting documentary and poetic vision against each other. After another installment to Byron, Auden begins his series of prose letters to his "wife," Erika Mann, in which he discusses photography and travel writing. (Auden married Mann so she could flee Nazi Germany with a British passport; they never lived together.)

Coming between the two Mann letters is MacNeice's poem "Eclogue from Iceland." Another of MacNeice's chapters, "Hetty to Nancy," parodies the masculinity of conventional travelogues with purple prose and a comic gender reversal. Calling himself "Hetty" and Auden "Maisie," MacNeice gives an amusing account of a camping and riding expedition the authors made with a group of English schoolboys. MacNeice also comments on Auden's experiments with photography. Next comes the autobiographical fourth part of *Letter to Lord Byron,* followed by Auden's prose chapter addressed to Kristian Andreirsson, an Icelander. In chapter 15 Auden writes to his G.P.O. colleague William Coldstream, a painter. This culminating attempt to represent Iceland employs a highly self-conscious, disjointed form that simulates the unedited rushes of a documentary film. The book's final chapters are the last segment of *Letter to Lord Byron* and Auden and MacNeice's terza rima "Last Will and Testament."

Visually, *Letters from Iceland* also reflects odd combinations of layout, materials, and styles. Most of the images are Auden's photographs, usually printed two to a page and identified with either straightforward or incongruous captions. For example, his snapshot of workers gathered around a bin of fish bears the caption "Herringgutting," but his shot of local citizens strolling along a street takes its caption from a line of Wilfred Owen's poem "Insensibility": "With paucity that never was simplicity." Several photo captions come from lines of Auden's poems in *Letters from Iceland.* According to Edward Mendelson, we can conclude with some certainty that Auden chose all the book's captions; a letter in Faber's files complains about his heavy handwriting on the backs of the photographs.[6] The images themselves focus largely on Icelandic people; we see them working in fisheries and in hayfields, traveling by bus and by pony, relaxing at sports competitions and at dances. Auden departs from travel book tradition by rejecting picturesque images of scenery; his only shot of Iceland's fabled mountains foregrounds a herring factory. He also plays with genre expectations by including shots with oddly dislocating perspectives, such as the low angle shot of an accordion player. Besides the array of photographs, *Letters from Iceland* contains assorted other illustrations: photographic reproductions of Icelandic artwork, pie charts and graphs that depict economic information,

and a fold-out map of Iceland's major roadways. While the photographs are scattered throughout the book (often but not always
near related verbal text), the other visual images appear in an appen-
dix. This discontinuous mixture of verbal and visual components
makes *Letters from Iceland*'s physical appearance more jarring than
the linguistic fragmentation of T. S. Eliot's *The Waste Land,* Ezra
Pound's *Cantos,* James Joyce's *Ulysses,* or Auden's own *The Orators.*

In one of the more perceptive comments about the form of *Letters
from Iceland,* George T. Wright argues that Auden's disjunctive text demands an active reader: "The audience as well as the poet is supposed
to think, instead of passively receiving picturesque descriptions. So
the book shifts from one kind of writing to another, from one author
to another, with the abruptness of fantasies or dreams."[7] Bringing into
play the book's visual images invites a revision of Wright's insight via
documentary film. Rather than dislocating travelogue with "fantasies
or dreams," Auden disrupts documentary's expository structure and
authoritative voice-over with unanchored montage. By creating
loosely edited rushes instead of a linear sequence, he challenges the
reader-viewer to construct meaningful relationships among the book's
competing parts. In fact, we can say that *Letters from Iceland* calls into
question the very possibility of representing that country.

Documentary Vision in *Letters from Iceland*

Auden invokes his documentary film experience on the book's first
page by touting "modern methods of communication" to Lord
Byron: "New roads, new rails, new contacts, as we know / From documentaries by the G.P.O." This allusion to *Night Mail, BBC: Voice of
Britain,* and other films about national communications points to
documentarists' ostensible purpose of promoting connections among
Britain's various citizens; in other words, documentary itself was a
new form of communication. As Samuel Hynes explains in *The
Auden Generation,* this kind of film "was to serve as an instrument for
spreading political, sociological, and economic knowledge, and as a
counter-force to the bourgeois propaganda media—the national newspapers, commercial entertainment-films, and public education."[8] One
can understand its appeal to the socially conscious young Auden,

whose poems attacking the status quo include a scathing indictment of two newspaper barons, Lord Beaverbrook and Lord Rothermere. (The poem, which begins "Beethameer, Beethameer, bully of Britain," appears in *The Orators*.)

Yet Auden questions as well as incorporates his generation's new discourse of social contact. He layers his opening lines about the G.P.O. Film Unit with two photographs that bear the captions "New communications" and "New contacts." Appearing three chapters after the related verse stanza, these snapshots present opposing scenes of social relations. "New contacts" depicts a group of young men talking behind a bus (fig. 7); their proximity and amiable expressions, along with the camera's fairly close position, coincide with the caption. But the pairing of text and image in "New communications" proves ironic (fig. 8). In this long shot of passengers standing beside an apparently stranded bus, the men are farther apart and do not face one another. The bleak, rocky landscape and seemingly impassable road make the caption even more incongruous; "Communication breakdown" would seem more appropriate. Auden's cross-referencing of poem, caption, and photograph reflects an underlying uncertainty about documentary representation.

Auden adapted much of the book's social vision and his photographs' style from the British documentary film movement. Among John Grierson's goals for both the E.M.B. and the G.P.O. Film Units was making the working classes more visible as a public image. As he writes in a defense of his early film work, "the workers' portraits of *Industrial Britain* were cheered in the West End of London. The strange fact was that the West End had never seen workmen's portraits before—certainly not on the screen."[9] Like his colleagues at the G.P.O. Film Unit, Auden found labor and laborers not merely suitable but necessary subjects to show his readers. The attention *Letters from Iceland* grants to industrial space departs from the picturesque, often depopulated scenery of conventional travelogues.

Some of the book's more polished photographs reflect documentary film's subject matter and style. In the chapter "W. H. Auden to Erika Mann Auden No. 2," text and image work together as Auden records his observations of Iceland's whaling industry. First he presents an emotionally charged description of how whales are butchered for market:

7. "New contacts," by W. H. Auden. From *Letters from Iceland* (Faber and Faber, 1937). (© by the Estate of W. H. Auden)

8. "New communications," by W. H. Auden. From *Letters from Iceland*. (© by the Estate of W. H. Auden)

I wish I could describe things well, for a whale is the most beautiful animal I have ever seen. It combines the fascination of something alive, enormous, and gentle, with the functional beauties of modern machinery. A seventy-ton one was lying on the slip-way like a large and very dignified duchess being got ready for the ball by beetles. To see it torn to pieces with steam winches and cranes is enough to make one a vegetarian for life.

In the lounge the wireless was playing "I want to be bad" and "Eat an apple every day." Downstairs the steward's canary chirped incessantly. The sun was out; in the bay, surrounded by buoys and gulls, were the semi-submerged bodies of five dead whales: and down in the slip-way ran a constant stream of blood, staining the water a deep red for a distance of fifty yards. Someone whistled a tune. A bell suddenly clanged and everyone stuck their spades in the carcase and went off for lunch. The body remained alone in the sun, the flesh still steaming a little. It gave one an extraordinary vision of the cold controlled ferocity of the human species.

Three photographs that accompany this passage convey a similar judgment. Arranged like a documentary film sequence, these images show that Auden understood the politics of framing and camera angles. The first, captioned "Whaling station during the lunch-hour," shows a large saw on a mechanical arm cutting across the background of whale pieces, rails, and ladders (fig. 9). By foregrounding the saw and making it the only diagonal line in the shot, Auden depicts it as a monstrous instrument of torture. Later in the book he explains to Coldstream that the saw "is for cutting up jaw-bones."[10] The next image, "Flensing by steam-winch," presents a group of men removing a whale's skin; Auden stands far enough away so that the whale dwarfs these workers, complementing his verbal comparison to beetles (fig. 10). Below this image is the third shot in the sequence; it shows what appears to be the same men and whale, but from an angle that makes the workers seem much larger (fig. 11). They have removed a cross section from the whale, and two of them are piercing its skin with instruments. Auden captions this photograph "The corpse."

The visual shift in perspective and verbal shift in tone manipulate the way we perceive the whaling station. Unlike his prose passage addressed to Mann, Auden does not undercut this documentary sequence by questioning his ability to "describe things well"—a signal

9. "Whaling station during the lunch-hour," by W. H. Auden. From *Letters from Iceland*. (© by the Estate of W. H. Auden)

that in this instance he trusts the documentary method for conveying "the cold controlled ferocity" he witnessed.

Auden also invokes documentary vision when he represents lower-class domestic space, a terrain the G.P.O. Film Unit began to scrutinize in the 1935 film *Housing Problems*. The best example is a photograph from the chapter "Letter to Kristian Andreirsson." With a classically composed shot, Auden foregrounds two children, a clothesline, and a boat in one of Iceland's shoreside communities; the children appear slightly below his frame's horizontal center, following photography's conventional rule of thirds (fig. 12). When paired with Auden's caption "What the tourist does not see," the scantily draped clothesline and close-set houses become signs of the children's poverty. This combination of text and image invests Auden with documentary authority by implying that he sees more than "mere" tourists do. He makes the same distinction in his remarks to Andreirsson three pages earlier:

10. Flensing by steam-winch," by W. H. Auden. From *Letters from Iceland*. (© by the Estate of W. H. Auden)

11. "The corpse," by W. H. Auden. From *Letters from Iceland*. (© by the Estate of W. H. Auden)

12. "What the tourist does not see," by W. H. Auden. From *Letters from Iceland*.
(© by the Estate of W. H. Auden)

It is an observation frequently made by bourgeois visitors that in Iceland there are no rich and no poor. At first sight this seems to be true.
There are no mansions like those in Mayfair, and no hovels like those
in the East End. Wages and the general standard of living are high in
comparison with other countries; and there is less apparent class distinction that in any other capitalist country. But when one remembers
that Iceland has an area larger than Ireland, a population smaller than
Brighton, and some of the richest fishing grounds in the world, one is
not convinced that the wages could not be higher and the differences
less. I saw plenty of people whose standard of living I should not like
to have to share, and a few whose wealth made them arrogant, osten-
tatious, and vulgar.

Note how Auden valorizes this eyewitness account by elevating his
observations above those of less socially conscious visitors. Unlike
"the invasion" of French tourists MacNeice describes "taking cine-photos
of four or five unhappy little native children togged up in pseudo-
national dress and standing in awkward dumbcrambo attitudes
against a blank wall," Auden strives for a more realistic representation

of Icelandic society.[11] We should certainly credit him for addressing so eloquently the issue of class division, reminding his British readers that they have more differences to overcome than their Icelandic counterparts. By representing the underprivileged in the double sense—portraying them and speaking on their behalf—Auden reflects documentary's progressive aims.

Yet his images of poverty also reveal the problematics of documentary's cross-class scrutiny, which are further complicated when the observer and observed are of different nationalities. Note, for example, how Auden's distance from the children allowed him to take their image by surprise—the girl awkwardly hitches up the back of her dress, while the boy peers tentatively from behind the clothesline. Unlike his close-up photographs of people who present themselves as they wish to be seen, "What the Tourist does not see" makes the children appear vulnerable. While the documentary artist may defend such images by appealing to "the human condition," Susan Sontag points out that they are not neutral: "Gazing at other people's reality with curiosity, with detachment, with professionalism, the ubiquitous photographer operates as if that activity transcends class interests, as if its perspective is universal."[12] Note also the caption's—and documentary's—assumption that scenes of poverty are more "authentic" than scenes of affluence, an interpretive bias underlying the populism of representing "plenty of people" instead of "a few." While thirties documentary film provided a necessary corrective to the affluent scenes in narrative fictional cinema, its cross-class gaze also drew rigid demarcations between the privileged documentarist who observes and reports and the human subjects who are observed and captured. Thus documentary representation falls prey to the very class divisions it tries to address, a contradiction that fueled Auden's criticism of the G.P.O. Film Unit.

Decentering the Documentary Observer and Viewer

Auden's borrowing from documentary in *Letters from Iceland* does not indicate full acceptance of that mode of representation. Four months before he sailed to Iceland, Auden used his review of G.P.O. colleague Paul Rotha's *Documentary Film* to assess the emerging genre. In his recent book *Claiming the Real*, Brian Winston acknowledges this review's importance as an early criticism of the documentary film movement's failure to question its governing assumptions. Auden saw a contradiction between advocating social reform and receiving financial support from government and industry, anticipating the opinions of many subsequent film critics. At a more fundamental level, his review points out the unequal class positions of observer and observed. Auden writes: "It is doubtful whether an artist can ever deal more than superficially (and cinema is not a superficial art) with characters outside his own class, and most British documentary directors are upper middle." This remark serves as a rejoinder to Rotha's assertion that documentarists have the "job of presenting one half of the populace to the other." Despite his progressive aims, Rotha's documentary model reinforces class division by assigning the privileged viewer's position to the comfortable classes.[13]

In John Tagg's terms, focusing the camera on the working class and underclass diminishes them because it "turn[s] on a social division between the power and privilege of *producing* and *possessing* and the burden of *being* meaning." Documentary, the new discourse of reality in the 1930s, presents itself as a means of selecting, classifying, and thus knowing the human material it depicted on the screen. Rotha's opening pages, in fact, declare that "the power of making things known that need to be known is the principal promise of documentary to-day." For Grierson, this function empowers documentarists by transforming them into bold explorers of indigenous cultures in the colonies, industrial terrain in Britain's North, and domestic space in the slums. Faulting earlier filmmakers for lacking "social confidence and an easy acceptance of the right to social observation," Grierson praised the G.P.O. Unit's progress in "giving each new slice of raw material a perspective and a life, leading us in each new adventure of observation to a wider and more powerful command of medium and material alike."[14] In other words, one could assert control over—even understand—social reality by mastering the documentary method.

Besides the filmmakers' selection through shooting and editing, documentary also asserts authority through the voice-over commentary that presents those under scrutiny as ready-made information to consume. Bill Nichols has addressed the effect of documentary exposition on human subjects in his discussion of ethnographic cinema: "Such films normally depict individual characters, but they focus their attention upon a level of abstraction beyond the individual. This is not only their strength but also their potential weakness. Individual social actors risk becoming no more than examples . . . with their value assessed solely by the quality of their exemplification." In other words, conventional documentary rarely allows its subjects their multiple social roles. An industrial worker, for example, seldom appears as spouse, parent, friend, citizen, but becomes instead "the coal miner" or "the furnace stoker." By fixing workers at the scene of their labor, the documentary film movement failed to show the richness of family and community life. Auden criticizes such restricted social vision by pulling documentarists from behind the camera and exposing them as de facto film commentators: "'We must abandon the story and report facts, i.e., we must show you people at their daily work, show you how modern industry is organised, show you what people do for their living, not what they feel.'"[15] For Auden, documentary creates an artificial order by excluding from its frame those aspects of social reality that would decenter its organizing eye.

Auden departed from his film colleagues by doubting how far documentary observation enables knowledge of one's subject. Toward the end of the review he states, "No reputable novelist would dare write his novel before he has spent years acquiring and digesting his material, and no first-class documentary will be made until the director does not begin shooting before he has the same degree of familiarity with his."[16] The G.P.O. Film Unit's rapid production schedule, the distancing class divide between observer and observed, and the limitations of expository structure all contributed to Auden's sense that documentary had thus far fallen short of its claims. What troubled him especially was the filmmakers' refusal to acknowedge these and other obstacles to achieving a more socially conscious vision. Given Grierson's low opinion of narrative fictional cinema—which often draws its plots from novels—Auden's linking documentary and fiction must have been one of the review's most galling statements. But for Auden, the lessons of *Letters from Iceland* reveal the permeable boundary between documentary fact and interpretive fiction.

In *Letters from Iceland* Auden often counters documentary's privileged gaze by blurring the line between observer and observed. He employs two strategies in decentering documentary authority—exposing the observer and dislocating the viewer. Each strategy employs modernist fragmentation in a more populist style. His first method appears in the odd chapter "Sheaves from Sagaland," a compilation of quotations from travel books about Iceland. Many of the travelers that Auden cites do not allow a counterperspective from the Icelanders; they subjugate native people and customs to their own sensibility. Auden subverts such appropriating vision by arranging the quotations under his own headings. His strategy becomes a political act as he exposes the travelers' judgments of Iceland as unintended self-portraits. For example, the section titled "The Natives" tells as much about the observers as about its ostensible subject. Here are Auden's reframed selections from Sir George McKenzie's *Travels in Iceland* (1812):

Concerning their lack of education

"It is not uncommon in Iceland for people of all ranks, ages and sexes to sleep in the same apartment. Their notions of decency are unavoidably not very refined; but we had sufficient proof that the instances of this which we witnessed proceeded from ignorance, and expressed nothing but perfect innocence."

Concerning their high-grade living

"Publications connected with practical morality are very common in Iceland, and several excellent books of this kind have lately appeared in the island, adapted chiefly to the use of farmers or those of the middle-classes; in which moral instruction is judiciously blended with amusing information in various branches of knowledge. The most valuable of these writings is a work called *Evening Hours*."[17]

Although he purports to assess Icelandic values, McKenzie inadvertently comments on his own—revealing upper-class British ideology to be repressive and self-righteous. His narrowly focused, aggressive gaze creates such hierarchical oppositions as decent and indecent, sophisticated and ignorant, English and Icelandic. Unable to perceive his own political investment in such labels, McKenzie sees native customs as inversions of more "civilized" British ones. In *Letters from Iceland*, however, Auden turns the camera the other way to allow us a look at the observers, exposing McKenzie along with his observations.

Reinventing Modernist Collage

Auden's excerpts in "Sheaves from Sagaland" also reflect the radical disjunction he uses to disrupt documentary framing and dislocate his reader-viewer. Warning that *Letters from Iceland* will defy genre expectations, he describes the book's fragmented format to Lord Byron:

> Every exciting letter has enclosures,
>   And so shall this—a bunch of photographs,
> Some out of focus, some with wrong exposures,
>   Press cuttings, gossip, maps, statistics, graphs;
>   I don't intend to do the thing by halves.
> I'm going to be very up to date indeed.
> It is a collage that you're going to read.

In this stanza Auden's initial letter enclosure analogy buckles under the accumulation of visual and verbal elements his book will include; he rejects proceeding "by halves" in favor of a collage format that resists binary structures. James Clifford has proposed that collage can offer a strategy for creating an alternative ethnographic discourse: "To write ethnographies on the model of collage would be to avoid the portrayal of cultures as organic wholes or as unified, realistic worlds subject to a continuous explanatory discourse."[18] Yet for Auden, a second-generation modernist, the collage forms that shaped 1920s modernism proved more problematic than they do for Clifford. The high modernist collages of Ezra Pound and T. S. Eliot exploded conventional ideas of poetic structure, but they also enforced a traditional hierarchy by grounding their allusions in the canon of Western literature. Quoting in the original languages rendered much of their work inacessible to all but a highly educated audience. In *Letters from Iceland,* Auden circumvents such obscurity and elitism by joining modernist fragmentation with documentary populism.

Auden's photo-textual collage reclaims the form as public domain. Demystifying this high modernist technique, he presents collage so that it does not restrict its audience to artists and academics; *Letters from Iceland* was a Book Society selection. Instead of relying on canonical passages from Homer, Dante, Baudelaire, Wagner—materials of high modernist collage—Auden often invokes both verbal and visual forms of mass media. His readers must construct their vision of Iceland from the book's fragmented accounts, just as readers form an impression of their own culture from the disjointed parts of newspapers and magazines. *Letters from Iceland's* public collage does contain some literary allusions—including the photo caption that cites Owen's poetry and the long poem addressed to Lord Byron (as much a public as a literary figure). But the balance of sources is certainly less academic than Eliot's in *The Waste Land,* which relies mostly on canonical texts. As Auden tells Lord Byron,

> Parnassus after all is not a mountain,
> Reserved for A.1. climbers such as you;
> It's got a park, it's got a public fountain.

A collage need not be an alienated artist's esoteric vision; it may offer instead a necessary and accessible way of representing the external world. In this sense Auden agrees with Rotha that "it is surely fatal for an artist to attempt to divorce himself from the community and retire into a private world where he can create merely for his own pleasure or for that of a limited minority."[19] While Auden borrowed from modernism to loosen documentary's expository structure, he also borrowed from documentary to engage modernism with a larger audience.

In *Letters from Iceland* Auden occasionally stops to ridicule high modernist techniques that alienate the general public. For example, in a stanza of *Letter to Lord Byron* he includes lines of German, French, Greek, and the fragment "glubit. che . . .," commenting:

> What this may mean
> I do not know, but rather like the sound
> Of foreign languages like Ezra Pound.

"Letter to William Coldstream" presents a comic portrait of MacNeice standing "on the quay muttering Greek in his beard / Like a character out of the Cantos—." Auden even includes a playful pastiche of *The Waste Land* in his poem "Journey to Iceland":

> Then let the good citizen here find natural marvels:
> The horse-shoe ravine, the issue of steam from a cleft
> In the rock, and rocks, and waterfalls brushing the
> Rocks, and among the rocks birds.[20]

Unlike Eliot's mythical, sterile desert in "What the Thunder Said," Auden's landscape reflects a specific location—the "natural marvel" of Iceland's wet, rocky terrain (which we see in several of the book's photographs). Its inhabitants are citizens, not fisher kings. *Letters from Iceland* borrows from and contends with Eliot's brand of modernism, which had been a strong influence on Auden's poetry during his undergraduate years at Oxford.

The book's most striking example of public collage is the chapter "Sheaves from Sagaland." Besides exposing the travelers, this anthology also inverts the high modernist collages of Eliot and Pound by featuring its quotations as the main text. His citation from Clifford Umbra's *Travels* (1865) provides a parodic analogy to quotation-filled works such as *The Waste Land:*

> Mr. X.
>
> "I discovered a curious fact about Mr. X. which accounted for that gentleman's occasional readiness in making a quotation. Every night he wrapped himself in a large grey plaid of which he was very proud; it had been, he said, his companion in the mountains of Mexico. I now happened to examine some scarlet letters on the plaid and, to my amazement, discovered whole passages from Shakespeare and other poets embroidered in red silk. In fact Mr. X. slept in a book and could always refresh his memory by studying when he woke."

Like Mr. X, the high modernist collage's author and reader cloak themselves in others' words to appear erudite. By contrast, "Sheaves from Sagaland" quotes mostly from lesser-known sources, and Auden undercuts his two canonical authorities. Shakespeare's "'Pish for thee, Iceland dog. Thou prick-eared cur of Iceland'" is hardly inspiring—especially when introduced with the heading "*The Immortal Bard proves that nothing escapes him.*" Neither does Auden spare much reverence for Richard Burton's unflattering remark about the Icelandic woman's "'habitual frown,'" which he frames with the heading "*The translator of the Arabian Nights gets the raspberry.*"[21] The "Sheaves from Sagaland" collage celebrates anarchic disorder, not literary authority.

Auden's photographs become another important element of *Letters from Iceland*'s public collage. Like the documentary films he worked on, this form of visual communication gave the poet access to a wider audience. Auden comments on photography in his second letter to Mann, stressing that the medium is not the property of an artistic elite: "It is *the* democratic art, i.e. technical skill is practically eliminated—the more fool-proof cameras become with focusing and exposure gadgets the better—and artistic quality depends only on choice of subject."[22] This characterization broadens the definition of both "artist" and "art" by emphasizing photography's availability to the masses. In the new visual culture that emerged in the 1930s, more people could participate in producing the photographic images that were becoming essential components of print media.

Auden experiments with several of his Iceland photographs, borrowing collage's fragmented perspective to confuse spatial relations. Several of his snapshots disorient not only the viewer's position but also his own, thus disrupting the authoritative gaze of both high modernism and documentary. The resulting instability can be quite comical. For example, the photograph captioned "The student of prose and conduct" shows MacNeice from the chest up looking through a tent flap, or probably through a man's pants legs (fig. 13). MacNeice as Hetty informs us that Auden "went round taking art shots of people through each other's legs," and Michael Yates (Auden's former pupil who was in the party of English schoolboys) recalls that Auden "would stumble about the lava like some amphibious monster taking the most extraordinary art shots: the backside of a horse followed by the guide Ari's bottom, a boot, distant views of half-hidden faces between our legs or under the horses' bellies." MacNeice takes up most of the photograph's left side, while the cloth in question cuts across the center in an uneven diagonal line. A lighter-colored object that also appears to be cloth cuts across the upper left corner. What exactly is MacNeice "studying" in this photograph? The caption comes from Auden's poem "Journey to Iceland," which characterizes various kinds of travelers and what they seek. Auden's speaker bestows on them their respective wishes, giving "the student of prose and conduct" these locations to visit:

> The site of a church where a bishop was put in a bag,
> The bath of a great historian, the rock where
> An outlaw dreaded the dark.

This list of attractions proves as disjointed as the photograph; both fragment their representations. But like the public collage in "Sheaves

13. "The student of prose and conduct," by W. H. Auden. From *Letters from Iceland*. (© by the Estate of W. H. Auden)

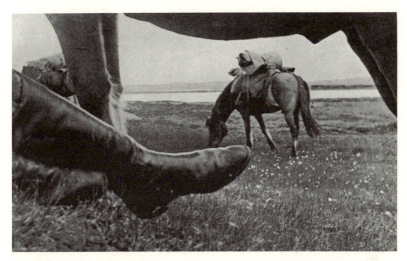

14. "Stella's boot," by W. H. Auden. From *Letters from Iceland*. (© by the Estate of W. H. Auden)

from Sagaland," such disorientation does not require academic knowledge to decipher; as John Fuller points out, these sites are standard tourist attractions in Iceland.[23] MacNeice, however, is not looking at any of these things—he regards Auden with a smirk. Blurring the line between observer and observed, Auden makes himself the object of the "student's" gaze and undermines his own authority.

An even more jarring photograph, "Stella's boot" appears in MacNeice's gender-bending chapter "Hetty to Nancy" (fig. 14). The title reflects a camp spirit in transforming his all-male riding party into a group of English schoolgirls. (Auden would inflect his second documentary travelogue, *Journey to a War*, with a camp sensibility.) "Stella's boot" depicts a pair of riding boots cutting across the foreground and the lower half of a horse across the whole top of the foreground; framed by this partial torso, an entire horse appears in the background. By showing only the boots, Auden masks the wearer's gender so he can attribute them to MacNeice's character "Stella." Auden's photograph also raises questions about the photographer's subject and position. Displacing the viewer, "Stella's boot" renders its subject indeterminable; only the caption makes us select the boots as a focal point. Where is Auden in relation to the boots? Possibly he twisted his body to include his own legs, which would make the photograph a fragmented self-portrait—another send-up of high modernism. This "portrait of the artist" can boast of fashionable fragmentation; yet the viewer needs no "footnotes" to appreciate its comic incoherence.

Poetic Parables of Alternative Vision

Auden's strategy of fusing modernist collage and documentary vision in *Letters from Iceland* shaped not only the book's overall format and its odd assortment of photographs, but also its poetry. With their invocations of "the camera's eye," the poems "Letter to R. H. S. Crossman, Esq." and "Letter to William Coldstream" reflect the camera-obsessed culture of the 1930s. *Letters from Iceland* appeared the same year as Christopher Isherwood's famous impersonation of a camera in his story "Berlin Diary," later part of *Goodbye to Berlin*. Storm Jameson's essay "Documents," also published in 1937, urged socially conscious writers to imitate their filmmaking counterparts: "Perhaps the nearest equivalent of what is wanted exists already in another form in the documentary film. As the photographer does, so must the writer keep himself out of the picture while working ceaselessly to present the *fact* from a striking (poignant, ironic, penetrating, significant) angle."[24] While the poems to Crossman and Coldstream adopt photographic and cinematic techniques, they depart from the decade's better-known invocations of camera vision by questioning its veracity.

"Letter to R. H. S. Crossman" has received considerable discussion; of the poems in *Letters from Iceland*, only *Letter to Lord Byron* has generated more. Crossman, a friend from Auden's undergraduate days and an Oxford don at the time the book was written, would later become a successful Labour politician. Most critics agree on the poem's preoccupation with perceiving and recording, concluding that Auden rejects "abstract" for "concrete" vision. For example, Herbert Greenberg sees Auden appreciating "the uniqueness of individuals and events," and Mendelson finds him contrasting "the real world of unique particulars and the imaginary world of abstract historical forces."[25] I find these assessments limiting in two ways. First, they divorce the poem from its context in *Letters from Iceland;* surely Auden's omission of these poems from collected volumes indicates their incompleteness without the accompanying photographs and other related portions of the book. Second and most significant, standard readings fail to question the dichotomy they establish with the terms "unique" or "real" and "abstract" or "imaginary," just as Grierson and Rotha fail to examine their assumptions about documentary realism versus studio fiction. Both adherents of "concreteness" reveal an underlying faith in representation to capture an unmediated fragment of "actuality." By contrast, Auden lacked confidence in realism; he found documentary to be a partially useful but ultimately inadequate means of representing Iceland.

Previous accounts of "Letter to R. H. S. Crossman" have not identified the external event that Auden's poem tries to describe—a sports festival mentioned briefly in his second letter to Mann: "The sportfest was a primitive affair. Some part singing by middle-aged men in blue suits with brass buttons which was barely audible, male and female high jumping, and a swimming race in a shallow and very dirty-looking pond."[26] Auden also represents the sport fest with two photographs captioned "Local swimming sports" (figs. 15 and 16).

Once again he blurs the line between observer and observed, this time with an upper image depicting the crowd of spectators followed by a double eye-line match of the swimmers (one of them turns his head over his shoulder toward the shore). The photographer observes Icelanders observing Icelanders. This sequence of images disorients because in order to align the spectators' and swimmer's gazes, Auden would need to reverse angle on the lower image; in cinematic terms, he has violated the 180-degree line.

An equally jarring sequence occurs in the Crossman poem, one that unsettles distinctions between concrete and abstract. The first stanza situates the sporting event in its distinctly Icelandic landscape, but Auden's ambiguous pronouns begin to blur this initial subject:

> A glacier brilliant in the heights of summer
> Feeding a putty-coloured river: a field,
> A countryside collected in a field
> To appreciate or try its strength;
> The two flags twitter at the entrance gates.[27]

Does "countryside" refer to the field's topographical features or to the local inhabitants?·Does "its" indicate the field battling with the glacier or the athletes competing with one another? Only the image of

15. "Local swimming sports," by W. H. Auden. From *Letters from Iceland.* (© by the Estate of W. H. Auden)

16. "Local swimming sports," by W. H. Auden. From *Letters from Iceland.* (© by the Estate of W. H. Auden)

the flags clearly evokes a human context. Such indeterminate descriptions complicate claims that Auden is advocating concreteness in this poem.

Our next clue that the Crossman poem's literal references are to the sport fest comes in the following stanza:

> I walk among them taking photographs;
> The children stare and follow, think of questions
> To prove the stranger real.[28]

This direct reference to Auden's activities at the event also comments on documentary observation, revising the predatory perspective of his photograph "What the tourist does not see" (see fig. 12). His on-location recording of Icelanders at leisure might seem to grant Auden the authority of making them "real" with his mechanically produced representations. But as the children's stares and dialogue reveal, the observing stranger's reality is also subject to interrogation. This reciprocity between Icelandic native and foreign observer also informs a photograph that draws its caption from these lines of poetry.

In the medium close-up shot "The arctic stare," an Icelandic boy peers under a railing at the viewer (fig. 17). The gazing boy is doubly framed by the joining rails' triangular shape, emphasizing his act of looking. Staring with wide eyes, he does not appear uncomfortable but coolly regards Auden, who seems to be below him. However, Auden fools the viewer with this perspective. If we turn the book on its left side to reorient the image to its original position, we see that the boy sits in someone's lap and looks *up* at the camera. Auden's choice in framing the image and in presenting it sideways empowers the subject, as does the caption "The arctic stare." Instead of privileging the photographer's eye, he repositions an image that would otherwise empower himself.

In other visual cross-references with "Letter to R. H. S. Crossman," Auden uses captions to contend with his images. Three additional snapshots from the festival draw their captions from the poem's third stanza:

> Nevertheless let the camera's eye record it:
> Groups in confabulation on the grass,
> The shuffling couples in their heavy boots,
> The young men leaping, the accordion playing.
> Justice or not, it is a world.

17. "The arctic stare," by W. H. Auden. From *Letters from Iceland*. (© by the Estate of W. H. Auden)

Again Auden turns to "the camera's eye" for a supposedly objective representation, which he invokes with the verb "record." But note the almost grudging tone of "Nevertheless," as if he senses that his words must compete with his photographs. In fact, some of the stanza's lines double as deliberately misleading captions that call both representations into question. For example, the photograph titled "The shuffling couples in their heavy boots" depicts a crowd of people greeting each other (fig. 18). While the caption suggests that they are dancing, only the couples in the right foreground adopt such a posture. The framing also crops these "dancers" at the waist, so the viewer questions the caption's authority in asserting that they wear boots. The photograph "Back to the hands, the feet, the faces" poses similar questions with its framing; we see faces but no hands and feet (fig. 19). Which form of representation is the "accurate" one? Roland Barthes's epigraph to *Empire of Signs* provides a good description of Auden's effect: "The text does not 'gloss' the images, which do not 'illustrate' the text. For me, each has been no more than the onset of a

18. "The shuffling couples in their heavy boots," by W. H. Auden. From *Letters fom Iceland.* (© by the Estate of W. H. Auden)

19. "Back to the hands, the feet, the faces," by W. H. Auden. From *Letters from Iceland.* (© by the Estate of W. H. Auden)

kind of visual uncertainty."[29] Like the Crossman poem's confusion of "concrete" and "abstract" vision, Auden's opposition of photographs and captions disorients our vision.

Most critics anchor their claims about the poem's concrete vision in the artist's prayer of stanza 5—which they assume to be straightforward. Yet this stanza's call for seeing anew unsettles the kind of delineations we make between abstract and concrete, imaginary and actual:

> And the artist prays ever so gently—
>
> "Let me find pure all that can happen.
> Only uniqueness is success! For instance,
> Let me perceive the images of history,
> All that I push away with doubt and travel,
> To-day's and yesterday's, alike like bodies."
>
> Yes, just like that.[30]

I find this prayer highly ironic; surely it is not to be taken as a prescription. Auden frames the prayer with the almost comical "ever so gentle" artist and the reductive summation that begins stanza 6. (This artist figure anticipates the whispering poet in *Spain*, written eight months after "Letter to R. H. S. Crossman.")

More significant, Auden's gentle artist makes impossible demands on artistic vision. His prayer begins with a peculiar tension between the "pure" and the "unique"—the former implying a distillation of the latter into something like the images in Plato's cave. Auden's artist asks for both, equating the two. In the stanza's next line, the artist asks to "perceive the images of history," which is to see a representation twice removed from its referent. Such circular vision evades the literal object of one's gaze, conflating the disconnected "images of history," the engaged perspective of "doubt and travel," and the linear progress of "To-day's and yesterday's"—what we might call collage, documentary, and travelogue. Rather than achieving "uniqueness," then, this artist collapses plural perspectives into a vague rendition in which all is "alike like bodies"—a vision that anticipates the ambiguities of *Spain*. Unlike the gentle artist, Auden knows that vision is always mediated.

In fact, we can read the entire poem as an allegory of representation—one that demonstrates the inevitable intrusion of one's subjectivity on one's perceptions and, by extension, on art. In its final stanzas Auden extends his initial frame to blend the sport fest with Icelandic sagas, that week's events, human nature in general, and the crisis of fascism in Europe. He returns to the "glacier brilliant" of stanza 1, but its boundaries now extend in all directions:

> Until indeed the Markafljöt I see
> Wasting these fields, is no glacial flood
> But history, hostile, Time the destroyer
> Everywhere washing our will, winding through Europe
> An attack, a division, shifting its fords.

He imagines the glacier-as-History "Flowing through Oxford too, past dons of good will" like Crossman. Iceland's landscape opens into the broader terrain of the human psyche and European social change (*Letters from Iceland* contains several comments on the Nazis). This representation explodes the very idea of framing, exposing the limitations of both realist beliefs in concreteness and reportorial claims of objectivity. According to Mendelson, this passage shows that "the artistic price a poet pays for a resonant abstraction like History is the forfeiture of truth," but I do not read the glacier's transformation as a fall from grace.[31] Instead, I find that Auden's poem achieves a fuller representation of the sport fest and its surroundings *because* of its tensions. The plural images of the glacier undermine any assumptions that one of them qualifies as "truth."

Letters from Iceland's forum on representation reaches its climax in Auden's highly self-conscious poem "Letter to William Coldstream." Although Joseph Warren Beach dismisses it as "mostly an account of what the tourist had observed in a fortnight," this unusual poem focuses primarily on Auden's documentary dilemmas in constructing his photo-text. Significantly, he chooses as the poem's recipient a G.P.O. colleague who was also an artist; Coldstream, a painter, would later become a professor at the Slade School of Art. Documentary's socially conscious aims appealed to both men's artistic sensibilities, but neither stayed long at the Film Unit. As Auden notes in his poem, he and Coldstream were "suspected, quite rightly, of being disloyal" to Grierson's documentary movement.[32] While their colleagues waxed enthusiastic about the new art form's powers of social observation, these practitioners of traditional arts often found it limiting.

The negotiations with documentary in "Letter to William Cold-stream" are more extensive than those in the Crossman poem, referring to a number of cinematic terms as well as to individual G.P.O. filmmakers. Disconnecting his observations, Auden creates loosely edited rushes by dividing the poem into a series of events and a collection of images—what he calls "telling" and "perceiving." These sections correspond roughly to a film's sound track and flow of images, respectively. But whereas the sound track of a G.P.O. documentary typically organizes the images through expository voice-over, Auden's poem to Coldstream rejects such connectives. In this way the poem—and by implication the entire book—reveals both the layers of mediation involved in documentary filmmaking and Auden's final attempts to overcome them.

"Letter to William Coldstream" begins with a humorous opening paragraph exposing the arbitrariness of narrative conventions, part of the poem's section on "telling." Auden offers an account of what he, MacNeice, and one of the English schoolboys (Michael Yates) did after their camping expedition: "Now the three ride from Hraensnef to Reykholt, where they stayed two nights. Thence they went to Reykjavik and took ship to Isafjordur. Joachim was the vice-consul, a man well spoken of. He found them a motor-boat to take them to Melgraseyri in Isafjördardjup." By the end of the paragraph this stilted pastiche of Icelandic sagas gives way to contemporary, colloquial language, but Auden rigidly adheres to the convention of chronological order. He calls this exercise "a little donnish experiment in objective narrative." Of course, chronology is a principle of selection crucial to maintaining narrative's linear structure; narrative can hardly be "objective." The "experts" Auden parodies in the poem's next section fail to recognize the ridiculousness of holding together this series of events by chronology alone. One critic from the *Literary Supplement* cries that Auden's story lacks landscape while "the professional novelist" complains, "'Too easy. No dialogue.'" Another reviewer rejects the story because "'It's simply not Tolstoi.'" Their contradictory advice in pinpointing the crucial element in narrative writing undermines these conventions and justifies Auden's decision to subvert them—a textual maneuver that outflanks the book's actual reviewers and critics who, like Fussell, find that "the narrative is disturbingly discontinuous."[33] *Letters from Iceland* rejects the false order that narrative imposes on the world.

Recognizing the artificiality of one structural device makes Auden more self-conscious about using others. As with the Crossman poem, this awareness makes the task of determining and representing his subject difficult, but constructing the Coldstream poem becomes an almost crippling enterprise. The initial obstacle is how to begin:

> I'm bringing a problem.
> Call it as Henry James might have done in a preface
>   The Presentation of the Given Subject
> The problem of every writer of travels;
> For Life and his publisher hand him his theme on a plate:
> "You went to such and such places with so-and-so
> And such and such things occurred.
>   Now do what you can."
> But I can't.

How does one position the frame? The travel book formula, with its reliance on chronology and events, becomes another grossly inadequate means of organizing the book. Earlier, Auden had explained to Mann that travelogue proves unsatisfactory because "the actual events are all extremely like each other—meals—sleeping accommodation—fleas—dangers, etc., and the repetition becomes boring."[34] The Coldstream poem is an unusual place to elaborate on this problem of organization, since it appears in one of the book's final chapters. Conventionally, we would expect the author to construct a resolution, but Auden disassembles his text.

He investigates the processes of perception and representation by returning once more to documentary. In this final attempt to fashion the genre into a less confining form, he pushes its claims of objectivity to the limits by impersonating a camera. This exercise both assumes and rejects documentary authority. While it dispenses with poetic conventions in favor of a more cinematic order, it also exaggerates documentary observation to parodic proportions. Auden portrays the documentary method as some form of divine objectivity:

> Very well then, let's start with perceiving
> Let me pretend that I'm the impersonal eye of the camera
> Sent out by God to shoot on location
> And we'll look at the rushes together.

This deus ex camera reaches beyond documentary film's "voice of God" narration in an effort to wrench images from any kind of framing context. Earlier in the poem Auden had admitted, "The poet's eye is not one from which nothing is hid." But here he simulates the kind of representation a documentary might achieve if such an unmediated "on location" perspective were possible. As he reviews his photographs for *Letters from Iceland*, Auden constructs a string of images loosely connected by cinematic terms:

> Now a pan round a typical sitting-room
> Bowl of postcards on table—Harmonium with Brahm's [*sic*] Sapphic Ode
> Pi-picture—little girl crosses broken ravine bridge protected by angel.
> Cut to saddling ponies—close up of farmer's hands at a girth strap
> Dissolve to long shot of Reykholt school

The camera's eye is attractive to Auden because it allows him to connect random images and events while avoiding both the causal logic of narrative and the rhetorical logic of expository prose and documentary. Yet replacing chronological and spatial transitions with editing instructions still involves mediation, even though Auden attributes the editing process to an "impersonal eye." As Rotha asserts in his book, editing is the primary means by which filmmakers interpret what they observed: "nothing photographed, or recorded on to celluloid, has meaning until it comes to the cutting-bench."[35] Auden cannot avoid the mediation of selecting and arranging his images.

A pair of photographs and their related verbal texts reflect Auden's vexed relationship with Grierson's film movement. Appearing on the next-to-last page of photographs, the images become *Letters from Iceland*'s final visual comment on Auden's documentary apprenticeship at the G.P.O. Film Unit. The photograph that receives the most attention in the Coldstream poem simulates Grierson's *Drifters*, a film about fishermen for Britain's herring industry. It appears opposite the page containing this verse description:

> And here's a shot for the Chief—epic, the *Drifters* tradition.
> The end of a visit, the motor-boat's out of the screen on the left
> It was blowing a hurricane.[36]

Auden's photograph, also titled "Epic, the *Drifters* tradition," shows two oarsmen, medium close-up, and the head and shoulders of a man standing behind them in the stern of a small boat (fig. 20). We

20. "Epic, the *Drifters* tradition," by W. H. Auden. From *Letters from Iceland.* (©
by the Estate of W. H. Auden)

see the starboard in the extreme lower left corner, and a portion of
the sea in the lower right corner. The oarsmen look intent on their
task (neither one faces Auden), while the man in the back looks
grimly forward but seems unaware of the camera.

When we consider this image in the context of *Letters from Iceland*'s negotiations with documentary, there is more at issue than the
"ribbing of Grierson" that Cunningham points out. Auden's "epic"
shot shows a small-scale version of men battling the elements, a
dominant idea in *Drifters*. Pointing to the film's theme of "the ardor
and bravery of common labor," Grierson recalled "the effort it took
to convince showmen of the time that an industrialized fishing fleet
might be as brave to the sight as the brown sails of sentiment and
that the rigors of work were worth the emphasis in detail."[37] The
Coldstream poem heightens such "bravery" in Auden's photograph
by pointing out that he took the shot during a hurricane, and the
image reflects Grierson's spirit by finding its drama in the oarsmen's
labor rather than in the rising waves. Yet Auden's "epic" label places

this image in the category of false narrative orders that "Letter to William Coldstream" rejects. In fact, Grierson's much-cited definition of documentary as a creative *dramatization* of actuality calls into question his claims of social observation: ardor and bravery, ingredients of heroic characters, effect a social scripting of the fishermen in *Drifters*.

Although Auden offers Grierson his thanks and respect in *Letters from Iceland*'s final chapter, "Last Will and Testament," his allusions to Grierson in the Coldstream poem imply that documentary proves no more authentic than other representational strategies for organizing reality. He makes this point photographically by pairing his "Epic" image with a snapshot that also draws its caption from the Coldstream poem:

> Now going up Isafjördup—the motorboat cost 40 kronur.
> The hills are a curious shape—like vaulting-horses in a gymnasium
>   The light was rotten.[38]

In this shot Yates and MacNeice sit on top of another boat, leaning against a short wall (fig. 21). Cluttered with the pipe that juts in the center and the pile of luggage and equipment in the bottom foreground, "The motorboat cost 40 kronur" opposes a tourist's snapshot with the more polished allusion to Grierson, causing the latter to appear staged. Auden's photo-textual pairing also reflects the book's visual and verbal interplay by invoking Barthes's "onset of visual uncertainty." *Letters from Iceland* questions the organizing eye and narration of documentary films, just as it questions the judgmental gaze of travel books and the allusive fragmentation of high modernist collage.

After reviewing his series of photographs in the Coldstream poem, Auden points out that it lacks the structural devices that lend order and unity to G.P.O. documentaries:

> Well. That's the lot.
> As you see, no crisis, no continuity.
> Only heroic cutting could save it
> Perhaps MacNaughten might do it
>   Or Legge [sic].
> But I've cut a few stills out, in case they'd amuse you.

R. Q. McNaughton coedited *Night Mail*, and Stuart Legg served as a sound supervisor for *Coal Face*. As we have seen, Auden's film colleagues may solve his predicament by imposing Griersonian "heroic" editing, but he opts for a discontinuous collection of stills and rushes. The "crisis" *Letters from Iceland* reflects is not narrative climax but representation itself. In his introduction to *The Burden of Representation,* Tagg includes this kind of instability in his characterization of the 1930s, calling the period "a moment of crisis not only of social and economic relations, and social identities, but, crucially, of representation itself: of the means of making the sense we call social experience."[39] Crossing national, class, and generic boundaries, Auden discovers that his culture's principal means of organizing social reality—documentary discourse—cannot contain his observations of and interactions with Iceland. His precarious arrangement of the book's competing parts makes forming a cohesive whole deliberately impossible for author and audience alike.

I find *Letters from Iceland* significant because it reveals a more plural, more distrustful engagement with documentary than does the

21. "The motorboat cost 40 kronur," by W. H. Auden. From *Letters from Iceland.* (© by the Estate of W. H. Auden)

work of many of Auden's contemporaries. When Fussell complains about the self-consciousness in *Letters from Iceland* and *Journey to a War* and claims that "nothing is rounded off," he misses their value. Auden's self-consciousness arises in part from his desire to create equal power relations between observer and observed. Although he interacts both verbally and visually with documentary, *Letters from Iceland* foreshadows his eventual disillusionment with socially engaged art. Yet he also rejects the high modernists' social disengagement by addressing the world around him with pen and camera. Orwell points out the inadequacies of the high modernist gaze in *Inside the Whale*: "Our eyes are directed to Rome, to Byzantium, to Montparnasse, to Mexico, to the Etruscans, to the Subconscious, to the Solar plexus—to everywhere except the places where things are actually happening. When one looks back at the twenties, nothing is queerer than the way in which every important event in Europe escaped the notice of the English intelligentsia."[40] Because documentary remains our century's dominant model of socially engaged art, we should credit Auden with exploring its powers and limits in the loosely edited rushes of *Letters from Iceland*. Auden's public collage reflects the diverse, fragmented means by which we go about making partial, tentative sense of our world.

4

DOCUMENTARY AND CULTURAL MEMORY

Spain, The Spanish Earth, and Capa's Falling Soldier

LIKE MANY leftist writers of his generation, W. H. Auden felt compelled to bear witness to the civil war that threatened Spain's Popular Front government of 1936. Generalissimo Francisco Franco, backed by Hitler and Mussolini, led the Nationalist uprising that would defeat Spain's Republic by 1939. For Auden and his peers, the Spanish Civil War was democracy's fight against fascism. If the legally elected government could prevail, they believed, then European fascism might be contained to Germany and Italy. Yet the Western democracies responded with a nonintervention policy, prompting the Auden generation to find alternative means of coming to the besieged Republic's aid. The decade's sense of political crisis converged with its documentary impulse as socially conscious artists came to observe and record the escalating conflict. They made no pretense of being neutral observers and sought ways to support the Republican side with their dispatches, speeches, poems, films, photographs, and other representations. Some writers, like George Orwell and the English poet John Cornford, enlisted their lives as well as their art. The International Brigades drew volunteers from around the world to join "the good fight" for democracy. Auden had intended to drive an ambulance for the Brigades but ended up working briefly for a Republican radio station; biographer Charles Osborne points out that because "his broadcasts were in English and were transmitted over a radius of not much more than fifty miles, they cannot have been of the slightest practical use."[1] After spending two months in Spain, Auden returned to England and made his major contribution to the Republican cause.

Auden's *Spain* remains the best-known poem in English on the Spanish Civil War. Even Orwell, the poem's most vehement and most cited detractor, could not deny its importance; at the end of the thirties he conceded that *Spain* was "one of the few decent things that have been written about the Spanish war."[2] Many of the controversies surrounding Auden's poem take their shape from the exclusively literary contexts in which critics have placed it—the most recurring comparisons being to Orwell's *Homage to Catalonia,* Cornford's poems, or Stephen Spender's poems. There is, however, a fundamental problem with restricting *Spain* to this narrow orbit: Auden's poem, which first appeared in May 1937, was a relatively early Spanish Civil War text. In fact, he returned the page proofs to Faber and Faber two days before the bombardment of Guernica on 26 April—the event that inspired Picasso's famous painting and provoked international outrage among the Left. Published a year before both Orwell's testimonial book and Cornford's memorial volume (and two years before Spender and John Lehmann's collection *Poems for Spain*), Auden's poem entered culture at a critical point of the Spanish conflict. The fascist-backed Nationalists had increased their hold to just over 50 percent of the country, and the Soviet-backed Republicans had to expend more effort defending Madrid from ground and aerial attack. *Spain* reflects the instability and uncertainty of this historical moment.

Auden's poem departs from its literary companions not only in *when* but also in *how* it entered thirties culture—as a single-poem pamphlet whose proceeds went to Medical Aid for Spain, and as part of Nancy Cunard's two-poem pamphlet whose proceeds also benefited the Republic. (The latter edition, published in Paris, also included Raul Gonzales's poem "Madrid.") However much critics may debate the poem's degree of commitment to the Republican side, its initial circulation was undeniably interventionist. Because Auden had been to Spain—and had published a partisan dispatch shortly after his arrival in January—his contemporary readers would have expected his major Spanish Civil War text to be an eyewitness account that, as communist activist Claud Cockburn put it, said "hurrah for the Republic."[3] Yet such expectations reflect a misunderstanding of the poem's alternative model of socially engaged art.

We can better understand the cultural dynamics of Auden's famous poem if we compare it with two visual texts that circulated in July 1937, the month of *Spain*'s second Faber printing. The documentary film *The Spanish Earth,* directed by Joris Ivens, and Robert

Capa's photograph of a falling Republican soldier provide productive companion texts for *Spain*. Auden's time in Spain overlapped with both the film crew's and Capa's; he would also encounter them on his subsequent journey to observe the Sino-Japanese War in 1938. *The Spanish Earth*, the most interventionist of these documentary texts, first screened at the Roosevelt White House, where Ivens and Ernest Hemingway (the film's commentator) hoped to influence American foreign policy. Although the photograph had appeared the previous year in two French magazines, its 12 July publication in *Life* established its international reputation as a document of the war. Like many artistic responses to the Spanish conflict, these three texts were produced by antifascists who were—in varying degrees—fellow travelers with the Communist Party and whose targeted audience was the noninterventionist Western democracies (Britain, America, France). Auden had invoked Marxist revolution in several of his poems; Ivens had worked with filmmakers in the Soviet Union; Capa had worked for a French communist weekly. Although these artists' compulsion to visit Spain attests to their belief that, as Auden put it in a letter to E. R. Dodds, socially engaged artists "must have direct knowledge of the major political events," they found reportage a necessary but insufficient strategy for cultural intervention.[4]

The poem, the film, and the photograph all manifest the Spanish Civil War's accompanying crisis of representation that blurred boundaries between public and private, soldier and civilian, text and reader-viewer. While the Spanish Civil War motivates all three texts, it is not their sole focus. Auden frames his poem with the sweep of Western history; Ivens and his collaborators frame their film with the relation of people to their land; Capa frames his war photograph with the isolating experience of death. This balance of the general and the particular invites us to see how each text's universalizing tendency aids rather than impedes its cultural intervention. Although *Spain* and *The Spanish Earth* avoid the partisan labels and testimonial voice that we expect in "committed" texts of the thirties Left, Auden's poem and Capa's photograph blur the local contexts we expect in "authentic" images of armed conflict. Reading *Spain* in light of these visual texts enables us to see the poem's dual status as a Popular Front intervention of its own time and as a transportable image in ours.

Spain and Literary Criticism

My analysis cites the original pamphlet version of Auden's poem that Edward Mendelson reprints in *Selected Poems;* it is slightly longer than the later version known as "Spain 1937." Several striking features have made *Spain* one of the most distinctive—and most controversial—war poems of our century. Because Auden defers the poem's occasion until the middle stanzas, the Spanish Civil War becomes more fulcrum than focus—a crisis-ridden "To-day" poised between Auden's anachronistic survey of Western history ("Yesterday") and tentative formulations of the future ("To-morrow"). As he directs the poem's energies toward "to-day the struggle," Auden also disrupts his framing, declarative voice with five vocal shifts. Two individual and two collective voices ask for a superhuman intervention in the growing crisis, but the responding voice of Spain transfers the impetus back to them: "I am whatever you do." Then the declarative voice returns to articulate the rest of the poem, which counterpoints the decisive moment in Spain with an indeterminate future. In representing the war, Auden eschews conventional battle imagery by linking the International Brigades with natural phenomena ("the seeds of a flower" that "floated over the oceans") and by rendering the warring sides as psychological projections of our best and worst tendencies. *Spain's* conjecture about the war's aftermath is also unusual, giving equal weight to such unrelated activities as "the photographing of ravens" and "the eager election of chairmen." Not surprisingly—given the uncertain state of the war when Auden wrote the poem—*Spain* ends in medias res, leaving us "alone with our day" and our decision.[5] Anyone looking to the poem as Auden's definitive statement on the Spanish Republic must have been disappointed.

Besides their concurrence that *Spain* is the most significant English-language poem on the Spanish Civil War, Auden's critics have found little common ground over the past six decades. For example, Orwell associates *Spain* with "warmongering," but Frank Kermode asserts that "*Spain* is not a marching song or a recruiting poster." According to Stan Smith, the poem shows Auden "acknowledg[ing] his place as a partisan" in the Spanish conflict; according to Samuel Hynes, the poem stands out as "the least partisan . . . the least concerned with actual war." Whereas John Mander condemns *Spain* for its "Marxist dogmatism," Hugh D. Ford hails the poem as "Auden's renunciation of Marxism."[6] Such interpretive debates occur within three types of literary criticism on *Spain:* one that focuses on the poem's relation to other Spanish Civil War literature, one that focuses on its relation to Auden's beliefs, and one that focuses on its relation to its reader. My own emphasis on *Spain's* cultural work draws from all three trends, especially from the last approach.

Spender's introduction to *Poems for Spain* is the prototype for the first critical trend and its central problem. In characterizing this 1939 collection of poems, Spender faced the dilemma that would vex subsequent anthology editors—reconciling Auden's already famous but anomalous poem with other literary responses to the civil war. Except for Auden, the introduction's most quoted poets are members of the International Brigades (such as Cornford), who "both fight and write" for Spain. As Spender continues to assess the collection, a schism develops between poems that are "written from *inside* Spain" and Auden's poem, which "stands at a certain distance from the actualities of the war." *Spain,* in fact, is doubly distant for Spender because Auden's physical presence in that country proves "irrelevant to his poem"—thus separating it even from other nonsoldier poems such as Spender's own. In short, Auden's poem proves central to Spender's thinking about Spain but peripheral to most of the poems he selects. Valentine Cunningham's introductions to more recent collections of Spanish Civil War literature reenact Spender's conflicted position. In *The Penguin Book of Spanish Civil War Verse* (1980), Cunningham repeatedly asserts that Auden's poem failed Spain's test for "truthfulness in poetry," unlike Cornford's and Spender's testimonial poems. In *Spanish Front: Writers on the Civil War* (1986), Cunningham brokers a truce between Orwell's "I-witness" accounts from the battlefield and Auden's equally truthful reflection of Spain's "malleability" and "multivalence."[7] Whatever the comparative literary critic's verdict on *Spain,* Auden's poem always ends up in a category unto itself. By forcing a competition between *Spain* and testimonial literature, critics have ignored the poem's connection to other documentary texts of the Spanish conflict.

The second trend in literary criticism reads *Spain* as a political autobiography of Auden's beliefs. Instead of marking divisions within the body of Spanish Civil War literature, this approach assesses divisions within the poem itself. The most important exemplar here is Mendelson, whose close attention to the poem's form yields a series of conflicting elements: psychological illness versus physical eruption, natural metaphors of migration and generation versus "human metaphors of hatred and division," a "manifest argument about choice" versus a "metaphoric argument about necessity." Placing *Spain* within the context of Auden's career, Mendelson reads such formal conflicts as clues to Auden's own divided loyalties. This approach to the poem draws justification not only from Auden's psychological metaphors, but also from his later revisions and renunciations of *Spain*. When Auden reprinted the poem as "Spain 1937" in *Another Time* (1940), for example, he omitted the provoking, pivotal stanzas that linked "invading battalions" and the Republic's "people's army" to our own divided psyches—an alteration that drew E. P. Thompson's charge of "political bowdlerisation."[8] Auden tried to exert further canonical control by omitting the poem entirely from both *Collected Shorter Poems* and *Collected Poems* and by prohibiting Murray A. Sperber from reprinting it his 1974 anthology *And I Remember Spain*. If Auden so willingly changed and suppressed the poem, one could argue, then *Spain* must not have been "committed" in the first place. Yet in designating Auden's evolving beliefs as the determinant of *Spain's* ultimate validity and value, critics in the second group downplay both its initial role in fund-raising and its continuing circulation in cultural memory—often in the original pamphlet version.

A third and more recent critical trend focuses on *Spain's* relation to its readers. For David Trotter and for Smith, the key issue is not Auden's degree of engagement with the Spanish Civil War, but the poem's ability to make contact with middle-class readers who seek social change. In this framework *Spain's* striking technical aspects become strategic tools for eliciting a constituent readership's participation in Auden's attack on bourgeois social structure. The poem is one of several that Trotter considers in his discussion of how thirties writers and readers negotiated the problem of "going over." He finds Auden most successful in using the definite article to encourage first his coterie and then a larger thirties readership to "dissociate themselves from a moribund culture." Auden's readers activated the definite articles in his catalogs of bourgeois sickness by bringing to the poem "their own experience and their own guilt": consider, for example, *Spain*'s litany of "the medicine ad.," "the brochure of winter cruises," and "the chain-store"—three false cures. For Smith, *Spain*'s deconstruction of "the basic liberal antithesis" between public and private experience has the potential to effect change in contemporary readers as well. In this context, Auden's rendering of the civil war as a psychological projection is neither contradictory nor autobiographical; it is an interventionist polemic attacking his culture's "inability to link the particular personal, apparently private life to the larger movements of history and the body politic"—a condition that produced both fascism and nonintervention.[9] By reading *Spain* as a reflection of its readers, critics in this third group relocate the civil war's decisive battleground from the front lines of Spain to the contradictions of bourgeois society.

Just as these three critical trends sometimes overlap, my examination of *Spain* sometimes borrows from their perspectives while revising them to accommodate the poem's intersection with visual culture. I share with critics in the first group an interest in *Spain*'s relation to other Spanish Civil War art, but my own interest lies more in finding common interventionist strategies. Thus, in my analysis *Spain*'s fusions of public and private domain are not, as for the second group of critics, signs reflecting Auden's divided conscience, but Popular Front strategies linking audience to event. I build on the third group's interest in the reader by considering the poem's function as a heuristic device in cultural memory. By returning Auden's poem to the context of the representational shifts also at work in *The Spanish Earth* and Capa's falling soldier, my approach counters those who find *Spain* politically disengaged.

Spain, The Spanish Earth, and the Popular Front

On the surface, nothing seems further from a poem characterized as distant from "the actualities of the war" than *The Spanish Earth,* which contains footage of frontline fighting and bombing raids. The film counterpoints the defense of Madrid with the irrigation of barren land outside Fuentedueña, a village along the Madrid-Valencia road. Crosscutting, sound bridges, and voice-over narration link these communities as equal guardians of the new, democratic Spain; Fuentedueña's irrigation project will yield more food for Madrid's besieged inhabitants. Unlike Auden, who wrote *Spain* upon his return to England, the film crew produced portions of their text under fire with the International Brigades. Hemingway's sixth dispatch recounts bullets flying close to his and Ivens's heads at the Casa de Campo, and Ivens's memoir recalls the crew's reaction to "the first bombs we had ever seen coming in our direction" as they filmed an air raid. By contrast, Auden made a brief, unescorted visit to the quieter Aragon front, and his radio broadcasts were issued from Valencia (where the Republican government had moved to protect itself from Nationalist advances toward Madrid). As Nicholas Jenkins has pointed out, Auden's lack of Communist Party affiliations would have impeded his travel to any Spanish front, especially Madrid.[10] Ivens and his film crew, by contrast, did not face this obstacle—the director's close ties with the Comintern facilitated his access to the International Brigades' communist commanders stationed along the Madrid front.

Despite their radically different degrees of frontline contact, both *Spain* and *The Spanish Earth* intervened directly in the crisis by providing medical relief to the Republican side: proceeds from the film purchased eighteen ambulances for Madrid. This cultural connection compels us to see if these Spanish Civil War texts of 1937 bear further comparison. Thomas Waugh's remark that the film "became a cinematic hybrid in the uncontrollable laboratory of war and revolution" applies to the poem as well; the unorthodox structures of both *Spain* and *The Spanish Earth* have puzzled their reviewers and critics. C. Day-Lewis, a contemporary reviewer of *Spain,* noted the poem's "oblique approach to its subject"; more recently, Mendelson has deemed its opening "a series of disconnected tableaux with no relation to the present struggle." *The Spanish Earth's* contemporary reviewers found a similar disorder; for example, Archer Winsten of the *New York Post* predicted that the film's "large and diffuse" theme might fail to engage the audience, and Dorothy Masters of the *Daily News* declared it to be "without beginning or end, without continuity or order."[11]

By revising their respective genres—socially engaged poetry and documentary film—*Spain* and *The Spanish Earth* mark a historical time of rapidly accelerating cultural change, a pivotal moment that postmodern novelist Richard Powers has called a "trigger point":

"As with free-falling bodies, it seems apparent that such quickening change, whether evolutionary, cultural, or technical, cannot accelerate indefinitely but must reach some terminal velocity. Call that terminal velocity a trigger point, where the rate of change of the system reaches such a level that the system's underpinning, its ability to change, is changed."[12] The proliferation of socially engaged art in the 1930s reached such a trigger point during the Spanish Civil War. In the case of *Spain* and *The Spanish Earth,* representational and political maneuverings intersect in ways that promote broad coalition building. The crisis erupting in Spain placed new pressures on thirties representation, which these texts reflect through their indirect framing of the conflict. As the decade's socially engaged art shifted emphasis from representing workers to fighting fascism, a corresponding shift in Comintern strategy abandoned the earlier class-against-class agitation in favor of a Popular Front coalition of communists and other progressives. *Spain* and *The Spanish Earth* signal this paradigm shift by avoiding the partisan labels we expect in "committed" texts of the thirties Left. Instead of editorializing about the war, both texts employ a number of vocal shifts to construct discursive democracies that invite the audience's participation.

Neither text begins with images of the conflict at hand; they frame the war in terms of European history and of agrarian community, respectively. Although such indirect framings initially seem unrelated to the Spanish Civil War, they respond to the technological dimensions that would make this conflict a pivotal point in the history of twentieth-century munitions. As we shall see, each text's framing also contributes to its political advocacy. *Spain* opens with a panoramic sweep of European history:

> Yesterday all the past. The language of size
> Spreading to China along the trade-routes; the diffusion
> Of the counting-frame and the cromlech;
> Yesterday the shadow-reckoning in the sunny climates.

> Yesterday the assessment of insurance by cards,
> The divination of water; yesterday the invention
> Of cartwheels and clocks, the taming of
> Horses. Yesterday the bustling world of the navigators.

Although Auden's loose historical catalog defies conventional arrangement, references to technology advance in a more pointed fashion as "the invention / Of cartwheels and clocks" yields to navigational instruments and then to "dynamos and turbines" in stanza 5. Significantly, *Spain*'s opening survey often links technology with scenarios of colonial domination. Stanza 1 connects the expansionist "language of size" that measures Asia's goods with the dissemination of the abacus, and stanza 5 marks "The construction of railways in the colonial desert"—a resonant line evoking images like the African transport trains hailed in *Industrial Britain*.[13] By this point in the poem, Auden's opening survey has prompted readers to participate in constructing their shared past by filling in his definite articles with particular events from their own understanding of history; for example, "The trial of heretics among the columns of stone" could refer to the Roman Empire or the Spanish Inquisition.

Yet *Spain* allows less interpretive flexibility in its exposition on power relations, and it implicates European readers in the escalation of munitions technology that would usher in World War II. When the poem begins to focus on Spain as a "fragment nipped off from hot / Africa, soldered so crudely to inventive Europe," it figuratively brings home the violence of colonial expansion. For these lines refer not only to Spain's vexed historical connections to the Moors (who now fight for Generalissimo Franco as mercenaries), but also to the latest demonstration of European "inventiveness"—Mussolini's 1935 invasion of Ethiopia (his bombers now join with Hitler's Luftwaffe in Spain). By using the broader term "Europe," Auden indirectly links his uninvolved English readers with the well-armed fascist forces who threaten a democratically elected government—a technique that foreshadows his pivotal equation of those readers' fears with "invading battalions." But the poem will also present its readers with the choice of becoming, as *The Dog beneath the Skin* expressed it, "a unit in the army of the other side."[14]

The Spanish Earth also offers its indirect framing as a strategy for presenting the war to a noninterventionist Western democracy, and an evolution in technology accompanies the film's gradual introduction of the conflict. Like *Spain*, the film opens panoramically—in this case with a series of extreme long shots that depict the distant mountains and arid fields outside the village of Fuentedueña (fig. 22).

22. Opening sequence from *The Spanish Earth* (Contemporary Historians, 1937). (Courtesy Discount Video)

These images—and the agrarian-sounding title that precedes them—give no indication that the film will address the Spanish Civil War and advocate on behalf of the Republicans. Whereas *Spain's* opening survey employed definite articles to blur historical contexts, *The Spanish Earth* employs shots of barren fields to prompt images of the ongoing depression in America. As Waugh contends, "Ivens' Fuente-dueña peasants are first cousins of the exploited sharecroppers and drought refugees who people the photographs of the Farm Services [*sic*] Administration and the exposé photo essays" of the times.[15] In other words, the universalizing tendency of the film's opening sequence becomes a strategy for bridging the distance between America and Europe by establishing an emotional connection between viewer and viewed. In addition, *The Spanish Earth's* close-up of cracked earth—a direct allusion to the Dust Bowl film *The Plow That Broke the Plains* (1936)—signals the genre's shift from fighting poverty to fighting fascism.

Modern technology is conspicuously absent in *The Spanish Earth*'s first Fuentedueña sequence, evoking a timeless, peasant world. Most of the farming implements are made of wood or leather; metal appears less frequently in plow blades and wash buckets. As the sequence comes to a close, a sound bridge of rapid gunfire plays over shots of men digging ditches in the fields; William Alexander notes that this sound is the film's first representation of the war.[16] The sound bridge not only links the irrigation project with the armed defense of Madrid, but also emphasizes the clash of modern war technology with the villagers' world. When later images of machine guns, tanks, and bombers appear, the viewer is to understand that the Nationalist insurgents are threatening an essential way of life—a harmonious, agrarian community that is worth preserving. Thus both *Spain* and *The Spanish Earth* make strategic use of broad, indirect openings to give their respective audiences a stake in another country's civil war.

These texts also engage in what Waugh calls "the usual Popular Front practice of 'self-censorship'" by referring to both the Republican and the Nationalist forces in broad, nonpartisan terms—another strategy for enlisting a broad coalition of public support for the Republic. Although the film contains more combat imagery than the poem, *Spain* and *The Spanish Earth* share strikingly similar methods of representing the warring sides. In both texts, the defenders of Spain's Republic become a "people's army"—a term that would gain more currency as the war in Spain merged with the conflicts of World War II. Carefully avoiding the terms "communist," "socialist," and even "worker," Auden's poem and Hemingway's commentary code leftist egalitarianism in mainstream, populist rhetoric. *Spain* and *The Spanish Earth* also avoid naming the communist-backed International Brigades, even though each text gives prominent attention to this largely working-class army of volunteers. In the poem, the Brigades figure as a shadowy "they" who answer Spain's call to action, traveling from their homelands and "present[ing] their lives."[17] Auden's indirect allusions belie the fact that he originally intended to drive an ambulance for these same forces. Self-censorship regarding the Brigades proves especially noteworthy in the film because not only did the crew shoot its war footage with the Eleventh and Twelfth

International Brigades, but the commentary also names Brigade member and political commissar Gustav Regler in the rally sequence.

A similar self-censorship mutes *Spain*'s and especially *The Spanish Earth*'s invocations of the fascist-backed Nationalist forces. Whereas the closest *Spain* comes to naming the aggressors is calling them "invading battalions," *The Spanish Earth* refers to the Nationalist side as "the enemy" or, more mutedly, as "the rebels." During the second battle sequence, the commentary even acknowledges the Nationalist forces' bravery and tenacity. As Waugh notes, the commentary does not use the words "fascist" or "fascism" (although the latter word appears in subtitles of the president's speech). Although *The Spanish Earth* does not invoke inflammatory language to characterize the Franco-fascist alliance, the commentary and footage make it clear that German and Italian intervention has prolonged the fighting and destruction. In the aftermath of the film's climactic bombing sequence, for example, text and image conspire to force the viewer's recognition of Germany's role in bombing Madrid's civilian population. After the camera surveys the damage from this particular raid—employing a dynamic series of pans and tilts—the film transports us to the scene of a downed Junker plane. As the camera zooms to an extreme close-up of the fuselage, the third-person commentary becomes a first-person observer who anticipates his American viewer's response: "I can't read German either."[18] Pointed without being militant, *The Spanish Earth*'s commentary assigns blame to the countries who supply Franco's airpower, stopping short of demonizing them. By contrast, Spain is the only country named in Auden's poem, which indirectly blames its uncommitted readers for the escalating violence.

Although their representations of fascist intervention depart from some of the more confrontational pro-Republican texts, *Spain*'s psychological projections and *The Spanish Earth*'s understatement do not reflect a comparative lack of commitment to the cause. Other antifascist poems and films sometimes lashed out at the enemy to provoke outrage in their audience. In *Poems for Spain*, for example, two contributions by Auden's peers depict the "invading battalions" with biting irony. Rex Warner's "Arms in Spain" points directly to the fascists' destruction of that country, declaring sarcastically: "lest love should blossom, not shells, and break in the land / these machine-guns came from Christian Italy." The bitter ending to Brian Howard's "For Those with Investments in Spain, 1937" tallies the fascist forces and directs the reader's thoughts to their victims:

> So, while the German bombs burst in their wombs,
> And poor Moors are loosed on the unhappy,
> And Italian bayonets go through their towns like combs,
> Spare a thought, a thought for all these Spanish tombs,
> And for a people in danger, grieving in breaking rooms,
> For a people in danger, shooting from falling homes.

The American documentary film *Heart of Spain,* released shortly after *The Spanish Earth,* commands the viewer and indicts the enemy in its most dramatic depiction of fascist violence. During a long take of a Republican soldier's mutilated arm, the film's commentator utters this imperative: "Don't turn away—this is neutrality—this is nonintervention—Italian style."[19]

While some might argue that Auden's and Hemingway's more muted words do not meet the level of commitment in these more passionate, contentious texts, such a position proves problematic in two ways. First, Auden's and Hemingway's dispatches from Spain show that these writers were certainly capable of expressing a fierce partisanship. In "Impressions of Valencia," published in the *New Statesman* four months before *Spain,* Auden points to the order and harmony he sees among the Spanish people, then sneers sarcastically at those who justify fascist intervention: "This is the bloodthirsty and unshaven Anarchy of the bourgeois cartoon, the end of civilization from which Hitler has sworn to deliver Europe." In his seventh dispatch from Spain, Hemingway reveals his partisanship in descriptions of Nationalist air raids, providing gory details of civilian casualties and distinguishing between "legitimate" and illegitimate targets; his eighteenth dispatch refers to the bombers as "Fascist planes." Second, the less pointed references to the Nationalist forces in *Spain* and *The Spanish Earth* can be justified as calculated strategies for promoting the cause in a climate grown increasingly hostile to radical and even leftist activism. As Waugh explains, "Explicit political labels complicated the broad-based popular coalitions that were the mainstay of the Popular Front, as well as the effectiveness of Republican propaganda within the Western democracies."[20] His characterization of American fellow travelers "dodging domestic red-baiters, religious groups, and censors" also applies to England, where censors cut *The Spanish Earth*'s exposure of German and Italian forces because it conflicted with official nonintervention policy.

Because their texts were fund-raisers, Auden and the filmmakers sought broader distribution than *Left Review,* the *Daily Worker,* and leftist cine clubs. Fully expecting "accusations of purveying red propaganda," Ivens ensured that *The Spanish Earth*'s commentary steered clear of "any overstatement." As he recounts in his memoir, "Hemingway had to be careful not to use any tendentious material, providing, instead, a base on which the spectator was stimulated to form his own conclusions." This strategy mirrors Auden's well-known dictum in his 1935 introduction to *The Poet's Tongue:* "Poetry is not concerned with telling people what to do, but with extending our knowledge of good and evil, perhaps making the necessity for action more urgent and its nature more clear, but only leading us to the point where it is possible for us to make a rational and moral choice."[21] Note that neither strategy gives the audience full control of the agenda; while the film commentary must establish the "base" that shapes the viewer's response, the socially engaged poem must lead the reader from apathy to action.

In representing the Spanish Civil War, the filmmakers and Auden avoid anchoring their respective texts in a partisan, editorial voice, opting instead to filter the conflict through an array of voices. Whereas modernists of the previous generation had employed multiple voices to prohibit discursive unity in their texts—a technique we also see in *Letters from Iceland*—these pro-Republican texts employ multiple voices as components of a collective voice. In effect, *Spain* and *The Spanish Earth* construct discursive democracies that mirror, respectively, the noninterventionist democracies and the new democratic Spain.

In *Spain,* vocal shifts usher in the poem's transition from power struggles of the past to the current crisis. The first voices to interrupt the impersonal framing voice are those of two bourgeois individualists who refuse to acknowledge the war. While the poet retreats to woods and waterfalls and apostrophizes "'O my vision,'" the investigator examines "the inhuman provinces" of planets and microorganisms and wonders about his friends. Stanza 9 brings in the more engaged voice of "the poor," employing the poem's initial first-person-plural pronoun ("'Our day is our loss'"); they at least read the newspapers, but they wait passively for "History the operator" to effect social change. Auden then gathers these and other, implied voices into a larger collective voice as "the nations combine each cry," imploring "the life" to "Intervene. O descend as a dove or / A furious papa or a mild engineer, but descend." The Western democracies' assertion of powerlessness in face of the Spanish conflict reveals a fundamental dishonesty that Auden highlights by placing the charged word "intervene" within their collective voice. As Smith points out, "The various metaphors for this intervention . . . all suppress the real intervention needed—that by the Western democracies, whose policy of 'Non-Intervention' had, as they knew full well, doomed the Republic."[22] In *Spain* neither individuals nor nations can claim uninvolvement; their lack of action shapes the Spanish Civil War as much as Italian and German intervention does.

The fifth voice in the poem's transitional section, the voice of Spain that answers for "the life," underscores this central point:

> "O no, I am not the mover;
> Not to-day; not to you. To you I'm the

> "Yes-man, the bar-companion, the easily-duped;
> I am whatever you do. I am your vow to be
> Good, your humorous story.
> I am your business voice. I am your marriage.

> "What's your proposal? To build the just city? I will.
> I agree. Or is it the suicide pact, the romantic
> Death? Very well, I accept, for
> I am your choice, your decision. Yes, I am Spain."

Unlike the individualist, self-absorbed "I" of the poet and scientist, the voice of Spain emanates "from the heart / And the eyes and the lungs, from the shops and squares of the city"; it is an engaged collective voice that draws power from its constituents.[23] This discursive Spain rejects ineffectual uses of words that plead for superhuman intervention, reminding us of the discursive actions we take in everyday life (the "business voice" that effects transactions, the spoken vows that establish a marriage). By returning the impetus for action back to the nations, groups, and individuals, Spain challenges the previous voices to form a proactive coalition that intervenes on behalf of a threatened democracy.

Significantly, the framing voice that utters the remaining stanzas shifts toward collective pronouns that hold the capacity to effect social change. Unlike the earlier voices that disclaimed responsibility, this newly charged voice acknowledges its complicity in the Spanish Civil War: "*Our* thoughts have bodies; the menacing shapes of *our* fever / Are precise and alive." While our fears and greeds become "the firing squad and the bomb" of the Nationalist's "invading battalions," our "moments of tenderness" and "hours of friendship" become "the ambulance and the sandbag" of the Republican defenders. If we can sustain our collective actions beyond moments and hours, the poem implies, we have the power to shift momentum to the Republican side. The collective "we" sounds again in the poem's closing stanza, underscoring the urgency of our decision: "We are left alone with our day, and the time is short."[24] Thus *Spain's* vocal shifts enact the coalition building among Western democracies that could ensure the Republic's survival.

The Spanish Earth employs several vocal shifts to represent the new constituency *within* Republican Spain, gradually drawing the viewer into that coalition. Hemingway's commentary opens in a third-person, matter-of-fact voice that identifies images and provides basic information: "This Spanish earth is dry and hard and the faces of the men who work on that earth are hard and dry from the sun." Although this frame narrator will become the film's major voice, it does not subordinate the other voices that occasionally interrupt it; in fact, some voices enter without any introduction by the framing voice. Immediately after the opening sentence, for example, the commentary shifts into a collective voice of the men we see working in the fields: "This worthless land with water will yield much. For fifty years we've wanted to irrigate, but they held us back. Now we will bring water to it to raise food for the defenders of Madrid." This fluid passage from framing to constituent voice becomes a structural device in the commentary's construction of a discursive democracy. During the evacuation of Madrid sequence, the framing voice modulates into a collective voice of women ("But where will we go?") and then shifts again to focus on an individual woman ("I won't go, I'm too old. But we must keep the children off the streets"). Moving smoothly from groups to individuals, these vocal segues join Spain's various people into a United Front that, as the framing commentator says of Fuentedueña's citizens, works together "for the common good." Unlike the passive voice of the poor in Auden's *Spain,* these collective and individual voices in *The Spanish Earth* assert an indomitable spirit even when victimized; the village men, freed from aristocratic landlords, plan to reclaim their land, while the woman facing bombardment in Madrid calls on her fellow citizens to look after the children. The people of Republican Spain do not look to "History the operator" to solve their problems. As Waugh states, the film "counter[s] images of victimization with images of resistance and revolution," consistently portraying Spain's people "as agents of history, not its casualties."[25]

As with *Spain,* discursive action in *The Spanish Earth* becomes an integral part of the effort required to secure the Republic. The film employs two key images to represent discursive action: dramatic speakers who address the army, and a loudspeaker that broadcasts in the front lines. In the lengthiest speechmaking sequence, soldiers gather to elect representatives for an upcoming conference of Republican troops. As we hear portions of each address (all in Spanish except for Regler's speech), the frame commentator identifies the speakers and translates their words. These introductions underscore the film's democratic theme, pointing out that the "brilliant" divisional commander is a stonemason and the dynamic Parliament member is a typesetter. In other words, members of all social classes hold power in the new Spanish Republic. Editing also contributes to this integration, intercutting shots of the speakers with shots of the cheering crowd. The speechmaking sequence culminates with shots of "the most famous woman in Spain"—La Pasionaria—whose addresses on behalf of the Republic would become legendary for inciting people to action. Significantly, the final, close-up shot of La Pasionaria wipes to a close-up of the army's loudspeaker that, as Alexander notes, broadcasts her stirring words to soldiers in the field.[26]

In the battle sequence that precedes these speeches, the film features another key image of discursive action—"the loudspeaker of the people's army." Once in position, the loudspeaker becomes a means of maintaining army morale (it initially broadcasts uplifting music), a conduit between Republican soldiers and civilians (several sound bridges emphasize this point), and a participant in the defense of Madrid (one long shot balances the sound truck with soldiers filing through a trench). After broadcasting La Pasionaria's speech, the loudspeaker transmits across enemy lines a former Nationalist soldier's appeal to desert Franco and join the Republican side. Thus discursive action becomes a potent weapon for the Republic, intersecting with Spender's equation of writing and fighting in *Poems for Spain*. We can also read this theme as a self-reflexive device asserting the film's role in the discursive battle for Spain—a more confident sense of participation than *Spain*'s lines about "the expending of powers / On the flat ephemeral pamphlet."[27]

A final set of vocal shifts in *The Spanish Earth* employs personal pronouns to intensify the film's pro-Republican message and to promote active viewing. First-person pronouns emphasize the filmmakers' presence on the scene, while second-person pronouns position viewers as citizens of Spain's threatened Republic. In two of the film's battle sequences, the commentary veers momentarily from third-person narration to a testimonial voice. The first example, filmed near University City, contains a shot of Commander Martinez de Aragon that prompts a vocal shift: "He was a brave and skillful commander and he died in the attack on the Casa de Campo on the day we filmed the battle there." Besides establishing a connection with de Aragon that enhances the filmmakers' credibility, the shift to first-person also heightens the viewer's emotional response. As these words sound, we see medium close-ups of the commander going over plans with his men; the effect jars the viewer by telescoping past, present, and future. Invoking what Roland Barthes has termed photography's "that-has-been," the film preserves images of Commander de Aragon's final hours; we react to *"a catastrophe which has already occurred,"* struck by the insight that "'he is dead and he is going to die.'"[28] *The Spanish Earth*'s other testimonial "we" occurs after the Madrid bombing sequence. As the camera pans dead Italian soldiers who fought for the Nationalist side, lingering over their letters and other possessions, the commentary shifts again: "They signed to work in Ethiopia, the prisoners said. We took no statements from the dead, but all the letters that we read were very sad." Here the commentary exceeds even the camera's documentary authority, revealing that the filmmakers had permission not only to interview prisoners but also to inspect captured belongings. This degree of access was atypical for journalists and artists covering the war, further evidence that Ivens's Communist Party connections brought *The Spanish Earth* closer to the action.

Second-person pronoun shifts work to bring the *viewer* into the war, prompting audience members to identify with the people they see on the screen. Following the film's democratic principle, the commentary fuses the viewer with soldiers and civilians, with men and women. In the first battle sequence, a vocal shift enlists our empathy with the Republican soldiers we see fortifying trenches: "When you are fighting to defend your country, war—as it lasts—becomes an almost normal life." In the first Madrid sequence, the commentary positions the viewer alongside the women who await their food rations: "You stand in line all day to buy food for supper. Sometimes the foods run out before you reach the door. Sometimes a shell falls near the line and at home they wait and wait and no one brings back anything for supper." By pairing these vocal shifts with images of beset but determined Spanish people, the filmmakers compel their audience to recognize a shared set of values. American viewers should agree with the Republican soldiers that one's country is worth the fight and agree with Madrid's women that one's family is worth the risk. For Sidney Meyers and Jay Leyda, two contemporary viewers of *The Spanish Earth,* this identification was so complete that it carried over to the climactic bombardment sequence: "The bombardment comes. The bombs are on us . . . We find ourselves beside the dead, touching their feet, meeting their unseeing eyes."[29] The commentary's strategic vocal shifts make viewers constituents in the film's discursive democracy, a proactive coalition that unites audience and filmmakers with the people of Republican Spain. *The Spanish Earth* presents its viewers with an insider's perspective of the civil war and transforms them into imaginary participants, a dynamic that complements *Spain's* strategy of projecting the actions of its seemingly unengaged readers onto the conflict. For both the filmmakers and Auden, documentary's repertoire of authoritative, monologic voices proved insufficient for representing the crisis of the Spanish Civil War— whether the distanced, the voice-of-God narration of *The Plow That Broke the Plains* or the testimonial voice of *The Road to Wigan Pier.*

A Trigger Point for Thirties Representation

The Spanish conflict was in part a crisis of blurred boundaries. In many civil war texts, the event spills over its geographical borders to trouble the audience's "neutral" home country; Warner's poem "The Tourist Looks at Spain" captures this sense of unsustainable boundaries in a single line: "In Spain is Europe. England also is in Spain." By closing the distance between audience and event, *Spain* and *The Spanish Earth* reflect their decade's larger unsettlings of the boundary between "private" and "public" experience. Hynes has noted that by 1933, when Hitler rose to power, the spread of fascist violence in Germany, Austria, and Yugoslavia prompted an awareness among writers of the Auden generation that "no private world would be secure against the pressure of events."[30] Auden's war poem of 1937 reflects this collision through its voice of Spain that purports to be the reader's "business voice," "marriage," and "bar-companion"; in other words, the Spanish Civil War shadows the reader at work, at home, at leisure. *The Spanish Earth*'s first battle sequence fuses public and private during its handheld camera shots inside a ruined house in University City (fig. 23). Positioned between the Republican soldiers' entry point and their upstairs gunning stations, the camera crew captures a man en route to join his comrades. Unlike the sequence's heroic shots of soldiers climbing a hill and marching along the horizon, this one seems strangely dislocated—note how the intact mirror above the man's head and the partial picture frame at the right edge evoke a domesticity at odds with the shelled wall and uniformed soldier. The Spanish Civil War ushered in a new politics of domestic space that departed from documentary's earlier, more voyeuristic framings of working-class interiors. Instead of reinscribing the line between observer and observed, pro-Republican images of Spain's shelled houses unsettle it by showing familiar signs of domesticity made strange by aerial bombardment.

Virginia Woolf captures the resulting defamiliarization in *Three Guineas* when she describes pro-Republican atrocity photographs: "They are photographs of dead bodies for the most part. This morning's collection contains the photograph of what might be a man's body, or a woman's; it is so mutilated that it might, on the other

23. Battle sequence from *The Spanish Earth.* (Courtesy Discount Video)

hand, be the body of a pig. But those certainly are dead children, and that undoubtedly is the section of a house. A bomb has torn open the side; there is still a bird-cage hanging in what was presumably the sitting-room, but the rest of the house looks like nothing so much as a bunch of spilikins suspended in mid-air."[31] If the spread of fascism is not contained, such images imply, the viewer's home could be equally vulnerable. The decade's sense of impending social catastrophe forced a recognition that the individual and the social, the personal and the political, are ultimately inseparable.

The Nationalists' aerial bombardment of civilian populations became the technological trigger point of the Spanish Civil War, collapsing the traditional boundary between soldier and civilian that had shaped previous conceptualizations of armed conflict. Whereas Wilfred Owen, the Great War's definitive poet, had written bitterly of the civilian's sheltered life in "Apologia pro Poemate Meo," "Greater Love," and "Exposure," the new paradigm in Spain rendered such dualistic conceptualizations obsolete. With the citizens of Madrid—and Guernica—becoming military targets, representations of soldiers and civilians had to change.

Pro-Republican texts often blurred the soldier/civilian line in two ways: by portraying government soldiers in noncombat scenes, and by fusing civilian artists with the soldiers they depict. *Spain* reflects the first tendency in its images of soldiers at leisure, Auden's only direct representation of Republican troops:

> To-day the makeshift consolations: the shared cigarette,
> The cards in the candlelit barn, and the scraping concert,
>   The masculine jokes; to-day the
> Fumbled and unsatisfactory embrace before hurting.

As with Owen's poems, Auden's soldiers form a loving community, but their activities take on the characteristics of civilian life. In the middle segment of *The Spanish Earth*'s first battle sequence, we also see the International Brigades at ease—reading newspapers, eating meals, getting haircuts. Waugh's comments on these images apply to *Spain*'s as well; by stressing "the humanity of the Republican troops" through scenes of "everyday non-military activities," he asserts, the film implies "that the stake of the war is the quality of everyday life"—the same point that Auden makes in his tentative catalog of what "To-morrow" may bring.[32] Such images of soldiers as civilians counter the atrocity images of civilians as military targets.

A second way of blurring soldiers and civilians builds on this proactive fusion of public and private by rendering pro-Republican artists as soldiers who join in defending Spain's Republic. Cunard's two-poem pamphlet, *Les poètes du monde défendent le peuple espagnol*, and Spender and Lehmann's anthology *Poems for Spain* contributed to the sense that this was "a poet's war." In *Spain*, Auden presents "the poets exploding like bombs" to usher in the future, an image that intersects with Spender's assertion that pro-Republican poems "have a literary significance parallel to the existence of the International Brigade." Because film and photography required closer contact with Spain's front lines than did Auden's and Spender's writing, the artist-soldier analogy became even more pronounced for documentary artists. For example, Ivens conceived of his film crew not as figurative equivalents or auxiliary troops, but as "real" soldiers: "My

unit had really become part of the fighting forces, particularly with
the units of the International Brigades." Similarly, Capa would assert
soldierly comradeship with Spanish exiles fighting against the Ger-
mans in World War II; upon seeing the word "Teruel" painted on
their French tank, he would say: "I am one of *vosotros*—your very
own—and I myself took part in that ferociously cold battle."[33] Leftist
artists of the Spanish Civil War consciously enlisted their work as fellow soldiers who formed a coalition with those they represented.
This fusion of artist and soldier, of text and event, would prove crucial not only to thirties artists' sense of serving a cause, but also to the
insertion of their texts in cultural memory.

Capa's Falling Soldier, *Spain,* and the Transportable Image

If Auden's *Spain* is the Spanish Civil War's most famous English-
language poem, Capa's photograph of a falling Republican soldier is, as
Aden Hayes has asserted, its "most recognizable emblem." Published
in *Life* above the sensational caption "Robert Capa's Camera Catches
a Spanish Soldier the Instant He Is Dropped by a Bullet through the
Head in Front of Córdoba," this 1937 printing of Capa's photograph
had a worldwide circulation of a million and a half copies. The image
became a news item again in 1996 when new research countered
claims that Capa had staged its "moment of death." Unlike Auden's
more distanced perspective in *Spain,* Capa's proximity to the front
lines imbues the image with documentary authority. These Spanish
Civil War texts seem to share little except the controversies each has
prompted. Yet both have become, as Powers writes of a famous August Sander photograph, "a memory posted forward" that "implicates
the viewer [or reader] as a partner in that memory."[34] Because the
photograph and the poem blur the local contexts that we expect in
"authentic" images of armed conflict, they are transportable images
that can bridge the Spanish Civil War with future wars.

Like *Spain's* closing lines ("History to the defeated / May say Alas
but cannot help nor pardon"), Capa's falling soldier has symbolized
for many the tragedy of Spain's Republic (fig. 24). For example,
Richard Whelan finds it "a haunting symbol of all the Loyalist soldiers who died in the war, and of Republican Spain itself, flinging
itself bravely forward and being struck down." Similarly, Phillip

24. "The death of a loyalist militiaman," by Robert Capa. (© Robert Capa/Magnum Photos)

Knightley contends that "if Guernica became a symbol of Fascist barbarity, then the symbol of Republican sacrifice was . . . Robert Capa's moving photograph of a Republican militiaman, falling backwards, arms outflung, onto the soil of the Spain he had tried to defend." Yet while the photograph can provide frameworks for the war, it is in and of itself an ambiguous image. As Knightley comments, "The terrain in the photograph tells us nothing; it could be anywhere."[35] Paradoxically, Capa's isolating the falling soldier from framing contexts gives the photograph both its vexing uncertainties and its affective power.

Though some would argue that any photograph has elements of instability, this combat photograph raises a number of troubling questions. Its slightly blurred focus gives the sense that Capa took it while under fire, inflecting the image with authenticity in the same way that the shakiness of the handheld camera does for figure 23. Yet these same qualities make the soldier's facial expression difficult to read. If he is indeed registering "the shock of being hit by an enemy bullet" as Whelan speculates, then his closed eyes and flat mouth appear curiously calm—even tranquil.[36] If the *Life* caption is correct in asserting that the bullet is passing through the militiaman's head, then the photograph's only sign of such an injury is the dark shape that appears just above the top of his head, roughly between the ears and the eyebrows. Is this a clot of blood exiting the skull, or is it a decoration on the cap that the soldier wears? In any case, the militiaman's head appears to remain intact, and the visible portion of his stark white shirt is free of bloodstains. Capa's framing prompts an additional question: Given its horizontal width, why do no other soldiers appear on the hillside? Varying accounts of exactly what Capa photographed have prompted some (most notably Knightley) to doubt the image's veracity.

While *Spain* has fueled critical controversies over Auden's political position on the war, Capa's falling soldier has fueled debates over the photographer's physical position at the scene. From Knightley's and Whelan's research we can extract three competing narratives of how Capa came to take the picture. In one account, the photographer was in a trench with several Republican soldiers under machine-gun fire. As some of the men attempted to charge the gunners' position, Capa held up his camera the moment he heard fire—catching one soldier as he was killed. This narrative is doubtful not only because such a blind shot would be uncanny luck, but also because the isolated soldier does not appear to be part of a group. Another scenario has Capa stranded in a trench with just one soldier, who grew impatient and decided to escape; the photographer followed the soldier out of the trench and snapped his picture as the two of them fell backward in response to gunfire, which killed the soldier. This narrative would explain the soldier's isolation in the frame, but it does not answer the questions about his facial expression. Still another account claims that the image comes from a sequence of staged maneuvers that Capa photographed; in other words, the "moment of death" is not what it appears to be. Yet given the need to recruit reinforcements against the insurgents, why would defenders of Spain's Republic fake their deaths for a photojournalist? Many of the details behind the photograph's production will probably remain a mystery. For Whelan this uncertainty does not diminish its value; in his 1986 biography of Capa, he chooses emblematic over documentary functions by asserting that "the picture's greatness ultimately lies in its symbolic implications, not in its literal accuracy as a report on the death of a particular man."[37]

Now, sixty years after Capa's photograph was made, a Spanish veteran's research and a British journalist's follow-up have identified the falling soldier as a young millworker, Federico Borrell Garcia. The photograph's emblematic function proves crucial to this documentary recovery, a process I find suggestive for thinking about *Spain's* role in cultural memory. According to the *Observer,* the veteran (Mario Brotons) "had read numerous books on the subject" and "kept coming across Capa's historic picture." The terrain and especially the soldier's cartridge belt and harness triggered Brotons's memory, prompting him to investigate local records and military archives until he had linked the famous photograph to Garcia. Rita Grosvenor, the journalist, then recovered another layer of the narrative through Garcia's sister-in-law, who remembered accounts of how he raised his arms at the bullet's lethal impact.[38] Were it not for the circulation of Capa's falling soldier as a symbol of the Spanish conflict, this story of a millworker from Alcoy might never have left the confines of his surviving family. Because of the way Capa framed his famous photograph, the fact that the falling soldier now has a name does not preclude its powerful resonance in other contexts. Noel Buckner, Mary Dore, and Sam Sills make effective use of the image in their documentary film *The Good Fight,* which chronicles American veterans of the Spanish Civil War. Capa's falling soldier appears between shots of Bill Bailey as he recalls being two feet away from a comrade downed by a bullet in the jaw. Cultural and personal memories intersect through the reproduction and consumption of Capa's photograph, triggering stories that allow us to reconstruct the larger narrative of our collective history.

Auden's poem is not photographic in the documentary sense, yet it shares with Capa's falling soldier the capacity to surround itself with multiple narratives. Like the photograph's transportable framing that, as Jean Lacouture has suggested, makes it an "ideograph" of the Spanish Civil War, *Spain's* layered images have made the poem a recurring heuristic device. In his introduction to *Spanish Front,* for example, Cunningham invokes *Spain* eight times to frame his discussion of the conflict and its literature. Hugh Thomas's history of the Spanish Civil War—which includes Capa's image under the symbolic caption "Death in Action"—quotes extensively from *Spain* to illustrate several ideas: the general mood in England, the centrality of the war for leftist intellectuals, and the conflict's urgency for volunteers of the International Brigades. In the third use of the poem, Thomas cites five stanzas of Auden's "still irresistible" words to introduce his discussion of the Brigades, beginning with these lines:

Many have heard it on remote peninsulas,
On sleepy plains, in the aberrant fishermen's islands
    Or the corrupt heart of the city,
Have heard and migrated like gulls or the seeds of a flower.

They clung like burrs to the long expresses that lurch
Through the unjust lands, through the night, through the alpine tunnel;
    They floated over the oceans;
They walked the passes. All presented their lives.

On that arid square, that fragment nipped off from hot
Africa, soldered so crudely to inventive Europe;
    On that tableland scored by rivers,
Our thoughts have bodies; the menacing shapes of our fever

Are precise and alive.[39]

Decidedly nonreportorial, Auden's definite articles, natural metaphors, and psychological projections open his poem to its readers' recollections and interpretations of the Spanish Civil War. And to a greater extent than Capa's falling soldier, *Spain* has the capacity to bridge its historical moment with crises of our own time. This dynamic plays out in the previously cited news article from the *Herald,* in which Ian Bell quotes the poem's closing lines to press for European intervention in Bosnia's civil war.

The cultural circulation of both Capa's falling soldier and Auden's *Spain* mirrors John Berger's call for socially responsible uses of photography that respect the "radial" laws of memory, through which the various manifestations of these texts become "an enormous number of associations all leading to the same event." Just as Powers's idea of a photographic "memory posted forward" requires our partnership as viewers to activate its full range of meanings, so does Berger's alternative use of photographs: "A radial system has to be constructed around the photograph so that it may be seen in terms which are simultaneously personal, political, economic, dramatic, everyday and historic."

When an image achieves this social layering, Berger argues, "it acquires something of the surprising conclusiveness of that which *was* and *is*"—transcending distinctions between public and private images. Smith describes the cultural work of *Spain* in a similar fashion, asserting that it "acknowledg[es] its own historicity" by drawing contemporary readers into its forward-looking lines about the role of history: "The text still interpellates us, as readers, into this history. It invites, that is, our own interventions." In Auden's transportable text, the decisive moment that his generation faced in Spain intersects with the decisive moments that confront us in a world still fraught with injustice and violence.[40]

Margot Heinemann, who lost her lover John Cornford to the Spanish conflict, has written that poetry "can outlast memory and transcend lying." Commenting on Spanish Civil War poetry in particular, she concludes: "Those who fail to learn from history are doomed to repeat it. But poetry, which reaches deep into the language we think in and the way we think, keeps something alive from the past."[41] Through the soundings and resoundings of its words, Auden's *Spain* has become part of the way we think about the war it represents. When I asked one modern poetry class why they thought Auden's poem remains the most famous Spanish Civil War poem in English, my undergraduate students offered some uncanny responses about *Spain*'s ability to involve its readers. One student contended that it "allows for a wealth of interpretations and discussions," and another concurred that the poem invites active reflection: "I think that Auden addresses the issue of the Spanish Civil War in a thoughtful and provoking manner. For example, he seems to delve more deeply into the underlying conflict of why the event took place and what those involved struggled over in their own minds. . . . There are no easy answers in Auden's account, which is more a part of reality than an easy black and white issue. War is confusion and Auden gives the entire spectrum of this chaos." As the next generation to inherit these quotable words, these young men and women may find that *Spain* will offer them strategies for coming to terms with global conflict in the next century.

5

DOCUMENTARY DILEMMAS

Shifting Fronts in *Journey to a War*

A YEAR after writing his dispatch from Valencia in January 1937, W. H. Auden once more set off to witness a world in crisis, this time traveling with Christopher Isherwood to an embattled China. For communists and their sympathizers on the Left, the Sino-Japanese War declared in 1937 was becoming another United Front against fascist aggression. Japan had seized Manchuria in 1931 and was expanding its territory in eastern China at the time Auden and Isherwood arrived. Their six months' visit occurred during a successful period for the Japanese, who were occupying several major cities, controlling the northern railways, and launching numerous bombing raids. China was also beset by internal struggles between communists and the Nationalist government, headed by Chiang Kai-shek (whom the English authors met and photographed).

Unlike the continuing Spanish conflict, China's war did not draw large numbers of international observers and literary responses. In setting off for this more distant front, Auden sought more maneuvering room for coming to terms with dominant documentary practice—especially its construction of masculinity. Textually and physically, he had thwarted his audience's expectations by not producing a frontline account of the Spanish Civil War. Isherwood reflected the anxiety of measuring up to Spain's "star literary observers" by asking, "How could one compete with Hemingway and Malraux?" The Sino-Japanese War appeared to offer Auden a blank page for inscribing what would become his final efforts at reportage and documentary representation: three collaborative essays and the coauthored book *Journey to a War* (1939). According to Isherwood's memoir,

Auden declared upon their departure that "'we'll have a war all of our very own.'"[1]

The text of *Journey to a War* enacts two "journeys," a literal one and a metaphoric one. Literally, it depicts Auden and Isherwood trying to reach the front of the Sino-Japanese War so they can understand and represent this international conflict. Finding the front would also validate them as documentary men, but this literal journey is constantly thwarted. For in seeking a focal point for the Sino-Japanese War, these gay Englishmen must negotiate competing models of masculinity and mediating signs of European colonialism. On the one hand, encounters with seasoned journalists, combat photographer Robert Capa, and especially the resourceful Peter Fleming make it difficult for Auden and Isherwood to sustain their manly performance. On the other hand, European embassies, businesses, and missions make it difficult for them to mark with certainty what is "Chinese." The resulting self-consciousness and self-parody disrupt their documentary travelogue, so that Auden and Isherwood's literal maneuverings also signify a second kind of journey. Metaphorically, *Journey to a War* enacts British documentary's return to its imperialist origins; this "journey" ends in the genre's deconstruction. Unlike their thwarted attempts to find the Sino-Japanese front, this metaphoric journey succeeds in locating—and exposing—the "fronts" of documentary discourse itself. *Journey to a War* exposes the lack of self-reflection in thirties documentary practice, most notably the failure of British documentary to confront its own heterosexist and colonialist genealogy.

Paradoxically, then, Auden and Isherwood's failure to construct an orderly account of China ensures their success in opening space for a critique of thirties documentary. A documentary text that does not cover its tracks, *Journey to a War* acknowledges and even foregrounds the absurdity of two Englishmen negotiating a densely coded and often inscrutable China. The unruly text plays out documentary's contradictions to the point of impasse, exposing its inability to apprehend the global conflicts that were evolving into World War II. Published as the documentary decade came to a close, *Journey to a War* marks Auden's abandonment of his culture's dominant model of socially engaged art.

Photo-Textual Instabilities in *Journey to a War*

Because it did not meet his expectations of war reportage, Randall Swingler issued this prediction in his review: "Many people will, I think, be annoyed by this book." Several contemporary and subsequent readers of *Journey to a War* found its discontinuous form a vexing issue. Unlike *Letters from Iceland,* this collaborative text does not intermix its verbal and visual elements into an overarching collage. No table of contents or list of illustrations prepares the reader for the book's shifting formats; instead, part-title pages divide *Journey to a War* into four sections: "London to Hongkong," "Travel-Diary," "Picture Commentary," and *In Time of War.* "London to Hongkong" contains six poems by Auden that portray the authors' entry into the East: "The Voyage," "The Sphinx," "The Ship," "The Traveller," "Macao," and "Hongkong." The 226-page Travel-Diary, composed by Isherwood from both writers' notes, covers the journey from Hong Kong to Shanghai and constitutes the longest part of the book. Auden took all but one of the sixty-one photographs in the Picture Commentary, which also includes two stills from the Chinese film *Fight to the Last.* Finally, *In Time of War* ends the book with Auden's sequence of twenty-seven often irregular sonnets, followed by a commentary in looser, three-line stanzas. Auden and Isherwood's text is, to use Samuel Hynes's characterization, "a discontinuous collection of parts in different forms."[2] As we shall see, the book's discontinuities occur not only among but also within its competing parts.

Critics have tended to discipline *Journey to a War*'s unruly form by invoking authorial and generic boundaries, pronouncing either Auden's sonnet sequence or Isherwood's diary the book's "primary" text. The review titles alone sometimes enforce such zoning, as in Evelyn Waugh's "Mr. Isherwood and Friend," or Geoffrey Grigson's "Twenty-seven Sonnets." Thwarting the expectations of traditional literary criticism, *Journey to a War* has provoked some rebukes for refusing to obey generic strictures. An exasperated Waugh, for example, decries the authors' "pantomime appearance as hind and front legs of a monster," declaring the impossibility of "treat[ing] this publication as a single work." According to Waugh, the diary is the book proper, and the publishers appended Auden's poems because poetry "will not sell." Lincoln Kirstein, another contemporary reviewer, concurs that *Journey to a War* "is a diary, with photographic and verse commentaries." Conversely, George T. Wright joins the majority of Auden critics by declaring that the diary "simply describes" while "the sonnet sequence and its verse commentary show us the *meaning* of their journey."[3] Departing from these critics, I will read the poems, diary, photographs, and captions against one another to show that none of the book's parts can claim central status. Because the sonnet sequence has received the most attention from Auden scholars, I will not offer another comprehensive reading of *In Time of War* (later revised as *Sonnets from China*) but will instead discuss how it contributes to the book's literal and figurative journeys. By contrast, I will devote considerable attention to the Picture Commentary, which has not received its due from Auden's critics.

Auden's Picture Commentary not only proves crucial to the documentary project of *Journey to a War,* but also contributes significantly to its textual instability. Although the book's status as a photo-text might lure us to believe that the pictures simply "illustrate" the diary, their uncertain relation to Auden's captions—as well as their often oblique relation to Isherwood's diary and Auden's poems—impedes this conventional approach. At first glance, Auden's Picture Commentary appears to be the most orderly part of *Journey to a War.* The photographs are labeled by captions as well as by page headings, which sector the Picture Commentary into three parts: "United Front," "Soldiers and Civilians," and "War Zone." Occasionally a label beneath the captions establishes additional links between pairs of images, such as "Provincial Governors" or "Missionaries." Auden's use of dualistic photo pairings seems to further the work of Western-style division and classification: north/south; communist/capitalist; Catholic/Protestant; officers/men; prisoner/sentry; intellectual/coolies. But he invokes this hyperorganization only to undermine it, thus questioning ideas of order that structure documentary representation and Western thinking more generally. For example, the captions "White Russian Restaurant Proprietor" and "Shanghai Business Man" bait us to assume a Caucasian/Asian dichotomy, yet both photographs depict white men in suits. In this context "Shanghai" ceases to mean "Chinese," so that the image not only subverts its caption but also comments ironically on Western imperialism.

The most unsettling photo-page in the "War Zone" section centers on two victims of violence, labeled "The innocent" and "The guilty" (fig. 25). Auden's gruesome lower photograph proves jarringly

25. Page from Auden's Picture Commentary. From *Journey to a War* (Faber and Faber, 1939). (© by the Estate of W. H. Auden)

ambiguous. In this jumbled mass on stony ground, we gradually begin to discern a dead man's right arm and chest emerging from rubble, alongside a hollowed-out oval shaped like the back of a skull. Immediately to the corpse's left, what appears to be a piece of clothing reveals, on closer examination, a face with an eye, nose, and mouth. The image evokes the frontline authority of a Capa photograph, but Auden confuses our response with his abstract caption, "The guilty." Was the person "guilty" because he was Japanese? Because he was a soldier? Or is Auden pointing to the irrelevance of such labels when faced with the atrocities of war?

When we read Auden's photograph against its caption and against other parts of *Journey to a War,* documentary representation is further unsettled. The most likely correlation in the Travel-Diary is this scene from Auden and Isherwood's visit to the village of Li Kwo Yi: "On a waste plot of land beyond the houses a dog was gnawing what was, only too obviously, a human arm. A spy, they told us, had been buried there after execution a day or two ago; the dog had dug the corpse half out of the earth."[4] But the brief description does not make reference to Auden's taking any pictures, something Isherwood often points out in the diary. If this passage indeed explains the image, serving as a displaced caption, then Auden has fooled us with this "frontline" photo taken far from the scene of battle. The lack of consistent cross-referencing between Auden's Picture Commentary and Isherwood's Travel-Diary often makes it impossible to determine the photographs' local contexts.

Occasionally, images from the Picture Commentary, Travel-Diary, and poems will align themselves into an unsteady triptych that further demonstrates the difficulties of accessing wartime China. One such triptych forms around the photograph labeled "The innocent," which depicts a war casualty lying on a board with one arm touching the ground. Covered with a blanket so that we see only the shoulders, an arm, and part of the face from chin to nose, this "innocent" victim compels our gaze with a mouth grimacing in pain. Again, the ambiguities of image and caption complicate our response by provoking several questions. Is the person male or female? Alive or dead? Does the cloth over the head shield the victim's eyes from the sun, or does it shield the viewer from his or her mutilation? Does the label "The Innocent" mean that the casualty is Chinese? Is a civilian?

The caption hides as much from the viewer as the blanket and head cloth do.

In the case of this particular photograph, the diary offers two tentative images for a triptych panel—a wounded soldier or a dead civilian. Isherwood describes several wounded soldiers from the northern front who had arrived in Kwei-teh "bandaged in the roughest possible way," noting that "often a bit of dirty wadding from somebody's coat had been simply stuffed into the wound." Later in the diary, an equally possible—and more disturbing—context presents itself when Isherwood describes five civilian casualties of a Hankow air raid: "All the bodies looked very small, very poor, and very dead, but, as we stood beside one old woman, whose brains were soaking obscenely through a little towel, I saw the blood-caked mouth open and shut, and the hand beneath the sack-covering clench and unclench."[5] Either or neither of these diary passages could represent the actual scene of Auden's photograph, but taken in tandem they blur the line between soldier and civilian in ways similar to Spanish Civil War texts.

The third triptych panel emerges in sonnet 17 of *In Time of War,* which brings the reader-viewer into the documentary frame. Like the ambiguous caption "The Innocent," Auden's unspecified "they" generalizes the Sino-Japanese War victims so that they exceed local contexts:

> They are and suffer; that is all they do:
> A bandage hides the place where each is living,
> His knowledge of the world restricted to
> The treatment that the instruments are giving.
>
> And lie apart like epochs from each other
> —Truth in their sense is how much they can bear;
> It is not talk like ours, but groans they smother—
> And are remote as plants; we stand elsewhere.

Several details, such as the bandage and the groans, correspond to the photograph, but here the central question shifts from the victim's identity to Auden's—or anyone's—capacity to empathize. As Michael O'Neill and Gareth Reeves point out, the sentence "We stand elsewhere" conveys "not only the perspective on us of those who suffer, but also, guiltily, our perspective on them."[6] With its feminine-rhymed quatrains and slant-rhymed sestet, this hybrid sonnet further emphasizes our failure to "only connect," as *Journey to a War*'s dedicatee E. M. Forster commands. (In fact, the hybridities and other irregularities throughout the sonnet sequence work against its presumed role of consolidating the book.) Again, the poems do not anchor Auden's photographs, just as the diary entries do not; together, these different media form tentative triptychs that question Auden and Isherwood's ability to represent the Sino-Japanese War. It is only through examining the uneasy interrelationships of its parts that we can read *Journey to a War* as a documentary text that enacts the genre's deconstruction.

Although previous critics have not integrated the poems, Travel-Diary, and Picture Commentary into their discussions of this book, my holistic approach is not without its critical forebears—both within and outside Auden studies. Hynes was the first to give a comprehensive account of *Journey to a War*'s verbal components, finding in its "mélange of confused, uprooted, fragmentary experiences" a mirror of the late thirties.[7] Looking beyond generic and publishing conventions, Hynes introduced the role of culture in the book's production. Gay studies and postcolonial studies have informed this chapter's larger discussions of masculinity and of imperialism. In the text of *Journey to a War*, Auden and Isherwood's position as gay Englishmen—as well as their ostensible object of study, wartime China—are unsettled through their late-thirties encounter. The resulting discontinuities merit critical attention precisely because they foreground the cultural issues at stake in these shifting fronts.

Journeys toward an Elusive Front

As he and Isherwood try once more to gain access to the Sino-Japanese front, Auden asks in exasperation, "How long . . . to the nearest fighting?" *Journey to a War*'s readers might find themselves repeating this question as they work their way through the book's lengthy diary and numerous photographs. Although the book's title evokes the dangers of frontline combat, the bulk of the Travel-Diary recounts, as Waugh points out, "sleeping-cars, mission stations, consulates and universities." Yet paradoxically, the same imperialist legacy that allows Auden and Isherwood such mobility also thwarts their access to the war itself. Hynes remarks that Auden and Isherwood's "two trips to the 'front' were farcically unsuccessful, and they found no battles to describe."[8] We would do well to take Hynes's cue in reading the word "front" with quotation marks, because the English writers journey toward the Sino-Japanese War only to discover their unbridgeable distance from it. Their lack of success in the conventional sense, however, enables *Journey to a War* to provide important insights into thirties culture.

Cut off from the "nearest fighting," Auden and Isherwood faced not only the problem of meeting their readers' expectations but also the challenge of validating their status as documentary men. Their dispatches published a year before *Journey to a War,* "Chinese Diary" and "Meeting the Japanese," show this struggle to establish documentary turf. Although the first article soon undercuts its heading "A Visit to the Front" by asking "Where was the war?" the second opens with the documentary swagger of a Hemingway or an Orwell: "If you have just spent four months in the interior of wartime China, visited two fronts, a dozen military hospitals, and the sites of many air raids . . . " By the time Auden and Isherwood construct the text of *Journey to a War,* they face the additional problem of having no combat photos for their book—even though a large section of the Picture Commentary is labeled "War Zone." Consider, for example, Auden's long shot titled "Japanese front line," taken in the daytime when no fighting took place (fig. 26). Evoking nothing of the war, this flat image of buildings across the Grand Canal clashes with its arresting caption; we agree with contemporary reviewer William Plomer, who wrote that Auden and Isherwood "made their way to the front, or perhaps we had better say the scene of military operations."[9] Such thwarted encounters with the elusive "front" yield tension-ridden representations, triggering the authors' scrutiny of their own expectations and motives. They challenge the validity that their culture assigned to war reportage, a subgenre of documentary that had gained more popularity with the Spanish Civil War.

Auden and Isherwood made two attempts to reach "the front"— first in the North and then in the Southeast. *Journey to a War's* images of these expeditions both conceal and confess the authors' lack of contact with "the nearest fighting." In the process, their self-deflation

26. "Japanese front line," by W. H. Auden. From *Journey to a War.* (© by the Estate of W. H. Auden)

also punctures the aura of male heroism that readers expected in the decade's war correspondents. Almost half of Auden's photographs are grouped in the "War Zone" section, seemingly echoing his insistence to military officers that "'a journalist has his duty, like a soldier. It is sometimes necessary for him to go into danger.'" The soldier analogy evokes the writer-fighter image that Stephen Spender and John Lehmann put forward in *Poems for Spain,* but *Journey to a War* quickly undermines this impression when we learn that Auden and Isherwood elected to hire private rickshaws for transportation to the front. The "Chinese Diary" dispatch includes a breezy aside recommending rickshaw travel "to anybody wishing to visit a battle area whose location and extent are vague"; this touristy tone shifts toward manly reportage when the authors point out that "if enemy planes come over, a single bound will land you safely in the ditch."[10] As we learn in *Journey to a War,* Auden and Isherwood did, in fact, face Japanese planes during their visit to the northern front, an encounter represented in Auden's photograph "Enemy planes overhead" and in Isherwood's Travel-Diary. The tensions between them reflect *Journey to a War*'s schizophrenic figuration of "frontline" experience.

Auden's photograph of Isherwood and a Chinese soldier clashes with its swaggering caption and its related portion of the diary. The soldier is one of their escorts from Li Kwo Yi to the Grand Canal front, where Auden and Isherwood managed, after several attempts, to gain military passes to the first-line trenches. While inspecting this portion of the "War Zone," the party is "interrupted by three tremendous detonations" from Chinese guns, and the escorts hurry their English visitors away from the front line in anticipation of counterattack from Japanese bombers. In the Travel-Diary, Isherwood recounts their departure through the bare fields: "From the north came the drone of approaching planes. The Japanese were out looking for the Chinese guns. They circled the sky several times, passing quite low above us. Whenever they came over, the soldier signalled to us to lie down. It was an unpleasant feeling lying there exposed in the naked field: one couldn't help remembering the many anecdotes of aviators' caprice—how a pilot will take a sudden dislike to some solitary figure moving beneath him, and waste round after round of ammunition until he has annihilated it, like an irritating fly."[11]

This verbal description suggests two types of dramatic shots—a tight close-up of Isherwood and the soldier conveying their tense situation, or a long shot in which the planes appear as a visible threat. But Auden's snapshot, taken from a middle distance, makes their situation appear absurd (fig. 27). Both Isherwood and the soldier gaze toward their left, which could indicate either that the planes are approaching or that they have already passed. Because the soldier in the foreground almost smiles, the latter scenario is more likely. Isherwood's diary points out that the soldier grinned "delightedly" after each Chinese shell exploded, obviously amused at his inexperienced companions. Although Isherwood writes that "Auden seized the opportunity of catching the two of us unawares with his camera," the soldier's posture—straight back, forward-clasped hands, torso turned toward the camera—certainly looks like a pose. And, we might ask, if Auden had the time to take this photograph, just how much danger was at hand? Carol Shloss declares two possibilities for photographers and writers who represent war: "As observers, they either shared the threat of death at the hands of a common enemy, or else their very safety forced them to confront their unarguable position as outsiders to the action they sought to represent."[12] Here Auden

27. "Enemy planes overhead," by W. H. Auden. From *Journey to a War.* (© by
the Estate of W. H. Auden)

and Isherwood present a third possibility by blurring these positions
through image and text. Simultaneously in *and* out of the scene, the
authors of *Journey to a War* represent staple images of war reportage—soldiers and trenches—in ways that call into question the
manly heroics of documentary realism.

Moreover, the authors' self-representation in their book leads to
self-scrutiny as they continue seeking the "front." We can see this
growing awareness most clearly in the Travel-Diary's account of the
journey toward the southeastern front, which Auden and Isherwood
undertake in the company of popular travel writer and *Times* correspondent Peter Fleming. As with their attempt to reach the northern
front, this one begins with warnings about danger; the divisional
commander even telephones from Meiki, the closest the English visitors will come to the southeastern front, to deter their arrival. As the
travelers enter the rain-soaked streets of the town, a group of citizens
greets them with a "Welcome" banner. Isherwood describes himself
and three of his Chinese companions entering on horseback "like

deliverers." But when the beleaguered divisional commander meets with the whole party and informs them that Meiki will soon fall to the Japanese, all illusions of self-importance vanish:

> Although very polite he couldn't conceal his dismay at our presence. We were tiresomely notorious foreigners, who might add to his responsibilities by getting killed. Our proper place was on a platform in London—not here, amongst exhausted and overworked officers and officials. We might have to leave, he warned us, in the middle of the night. The evacuation of the civilian population had started already. Touched, and rather ashamed of myself, I thought of those men and women who had wasted their last precious hours of safety, waiting to welcome us with their banner in the rain.

Isherwood finally understands that what he and Auden consider their journalists' "duty" is really a selfish imposition on those they supposedly aid with their reporting. Becoming part of the story did not make them heroic documentary men, but posed a danger to others. This is one point Swingler misses in his blistering review, which claims that one goes to a war-stricken country "to find out what is really happening and to report it or to participate," and then faults Auden and Isherwood for doing neither.[13] "Finding out" *is* participation, and counterproductive participation at that.

The Meiki experience casts new meanings on the denouement of Auden's sonnet sequence, which also expresses disillusionment over discovering that "all the apparatus of report / Confirms the triumph of our enemies." Sonnet 26 in particular glosses the account in the Travel-Diary if we read the "we" as Auden and Isherwood themselves, the "daring plan" of the sestet as their ill-fated expedition to the southeastern front, and the "work" in progress as their documentary project, *Journey to a War:*

> Always far from the centre of our names,
> The little workshop of love: yes, but how wrong
> We were about the old manors and the long
> Abandoned Folly and the children's games.
>
> Only the acquisitive expects a quaint
> Unsaleable product, something to please
> An artistic girl; it's the selfish who sees
> In every impractical beggar a saint.

We can't believe that we ourselves designed it,
A minor item of our daring plan
That caused no trouble; we took no notice of it.

Disaster comes, and we're amazed to find it
The single project that since work began
Through all the cycle showed a steady profit.[14]

The octave of this Italian sonnet begins by linking a series of structures whose time has passed—both in the span of history (as in an outdated class system of "old manors") and in the span of one's life (as in the passage from "children's games"). Thus far Auden follows the poetic strategies of *Spain,* but the octave grows more self-reflexive in its second half with the words "unsaleable product" and "artistic." Here the poem expresses anxiety over *Journey to a War'*s economic and political impact; on the one hand it might not sell, while on the other it might perpetuate documentary's penchant for romanticizing the dispossessed.

Then comes the self-scrutinizing turn at the sestet, in which the "we" narrows to Auden and Isherwood questioning their own assumptions and intentions. Because sonnet 26 is formally more regular than many in the sequence, its first pair of feminine rhymes (designed it, find it) stands out; significantly, the rhymes refer to Auden and Isherwood's constructing a dramatic "frontline" encounter but instead discovering an impending disaster and their own complicity. These feminine endings unsettle not only the sonnet's dominant rhyme scheme, but also the authors' own position. No longer "centered" by their male names and their sense of importance as war reporters, they bear witness to their inability to become writer-fighters and contribute to the defeat of the Japanese.

Auden's sequence of sonnets ends with us "Wandering lost upon the mountains of our choice," while Isherwood's Travel-Diary ends with the confession that "'One doesn't know where to start.'" Where was the war? After their final journey toward the front, Auden and Isherwood are disabused of the belief that war has clear focal points and dividing lines. As Auden came to understand on the road to Meiki, "War is bombing an already disused arsenal, missing it, and killing a few old women. War is lying in a stable with a gangrenous leg. War is drinking hot water in a barn and worrying about one's wife. War is a handful of lost and terrified men in the mountains, shooting at something moving in the undergrowth. War is waiting for days with nothing to do; shouting down a dead telephone; going without sleep, or sex, or a wash. War is untidy, inefficient, obscure, and largely a matter of chance."[15] In other words, the war is a decentered experience devoid of the man-making feats that structure linear plots—whether in novels, travel books, commercial films, or documentary texts. Once Auden, Isherwood, and their readers are devoid of frontline illusions, they can perceive how Western masculinity and imperialism interpose themselves between the authors and China.

Performing Masculinity in *Journey to a War*

While the failure to produce an orderly march to "the front" has motivated rebukes of *Journey to a War,* I see an equally determining factor at work in literary criticism—Auden and Isherwood's refusal to sustain a seamless performance as documentary (i.e., straight) men in their text. Theatrical tropes permeate unfavorable commentary on this book, ranging from Waugh's accusation of "pantomime" to Paul Fussell's more recent complaint that "uncertainty and frustration compromise the travel performance of Auden and Isherwood." Swingler expended more energy berating Auden and Isherwood's textual theatrics: "It is impossible to escape the impression that the authors are playing: playing at being war correspondents, at being Englishmen, at being poets."[16] In other words, Swingler finds a lack of *authenticity* in *Journey to a War* because Auden and Isherwood forthrightly acknowledge that they perform not only their profession, but even their gender and nationality.

Given the Anglo-American tendency to characterize gay men with such terms as "theatrical" and "stagey," I cannot help but wonder if the underlying issue for *Journey to a War's* staunchest detractors is the authors' supposed failure to measure up as "real" men. The unreality these critics find in Auden and Isherwood's textual performance assumes a heterosexual "authenticity" behind war reportage and travel writing that has been travestied; as Judith Butler has argued, "Compulsory heterosexuality sets itself up as the original, the true, the authentic; the norm that determines the real implies that 'being' lesbian [or gay] is always a kind of mimimg, a vain effort to participate in the phantasmatic plenitude of naturalized heterosexuality which will always and only fail."[17] When we factor into Butler's equation the heterosexism of thirties documentary discourse—in which "realness" means not only documentary's subject matter but also its dominant constructions of masculinity—we can see that gender is very much at stake for *Journey to a War*'s readers and authors. This text foregrounds the alternative masculinities that *Industrial Britain* and *Coal Face* presented less directly.

Part of Auden and Isherwood's difficulties in representing the Sino-Japanese War arose from their position as gay men writing within an established documentary framework. This position was markedly different from their earlier collaborations within the gay circle of the Group Theatre. We know from Isherwood's *Christopher and His Kind* that he and Auden had been occasionally sleeping together for a decade by the time they embarked for China. As Isherwood puts it, "They couldn't think of themselves as lovers, yet sex had given friendship an extra dimension."[18] Given the inevitable self-representation in *Journey to a War* and the possibility of readers' finding signs that the authors did not conform to "real" men, Auden and Isherwood risked being perceived as unreliable narrators of social reality. In response to this documentary dilemma, *Journey to a War* becomes—as Harold Nicolson's dust-jacket blurb for the American edition astutely noted—"the carefully gay account of their adventures." Critics who question Auden and Isherwood's political "commitment" in their account of China fail to consider the gender politics that the authors confront throughout the book. *Journey to a War,* in fact, provides a triple *coverage:* Auden and Isherwood cover (report) the war, cover (conceal) their sexual orientation, and cover (reperform) prior acts by straight men. This part of my discussion focuses on the latter two senses of the term.

Journey to a War's double coverage of maleness succeeds in exposing traditional Western masculinity as a documentary "front," employing four performative strategies. First, Auden and Isherwood at times perform what Butler calls the "necessary drag" of passing for straight. We can best see this strategy by considering what they omit from *Journey to a War* and by reading the book's signs of gay coding; Esther Newton's comments on the performance of "passing" shed light on these aspects of the gay Englishmen's collaboration. Second, the authors often respond to their position as gay documentarists in China by camping traditional masculinity, which we see in their self-representation in *Journey to a War*. With these methods of strategic concealment, the book's status as a gay text is sufficiently "covered" while still allowing space for critique; this interrogation occurs in Auden and Isherwood's third and fourth performative strategies, which reproduce images of patriarchal masculinity. In their third strategy, the authors highlight the constructed nature of masculinity by portraying documentary men they encounter—especially the theatrical Fleming. By depicting the consummate war reporter as consummate performer, they anticipate Butler's performative theory of heterosexuality and begin the work of what Lee Edelman calls "homographesis"—creating a text that both writes and unwrites compulsory heterosexuality. Finally, Auden's commentary to the sonnet sequence (which ends the book) rewrites history by critiquing the "great men" theory of Western civilization. These textual-sexual strategies work with and against each other to disrupt *Journey to a War*'s reportage of the conflict, the male heterosexual framework of thirties documentary discourse, and Western masculinity itself.

Journey to a War performs "necessary drag" through the play of concealing overt references to homosexuality while at the same time providing coded references to it. Engaging in a higher-stakes version of what Wayne Koestenbaum calls the "double-talk" of all male literary collaborators, Auden and Isherwood "give the taboo subject some liberty to roam" in their carefully gay account.[19] But they allow it freer reign in solo writings withheld from *Journey to a War*—Auden's poem "Passenger Shanty" (unpublished until Edward Mendelson's edition, *The English Auden*) and Isherwood's reminiscences of China in *Christopher and His Kind* (published in 1976). Each of these telling omissions glosses the coded references to the authors' homosexuality in *Journey to a War*'s Travel-Diary.

Auden wrote "Passenger Shanty" on the voyage to China in 1938, and it serves as a pre-text to *Journey to a War*'s strategy of dragging heterosexuality. Capa and *The Spanish Earth*'s cameraman John Ferno were on board the ship, and one stanza of Auden's poem notes the famous combat photographer's documentary and heterosexual prowess:

> The journalist Capa plays dicing games,
> He photographed Teruel Town in flames,
> He pinches the bottoms of all the dames.

Journey to a War also alludes to Capa's and Ferno's "bottom-pinching" and "endless jokes about *les poules*." By contrast, "Passenger Shanty" refers indirectly to Auden's sexuality through the rubber merchant's wife, who regards him with suspicion:

> His wife learns astrology out of a book,
> Says, "Your horoscope's queer and I don't like its look.
> With the Moon against Virgo you might be a crook."[20]

Auden uses not only the word "queer" in these lines, but also a form of the word "crooked"—his trope for homosexuality in his earlier industrial love poems. None of the poems in *Journey to a War* come so close to revealing homosexuality; in fact, we could read the sonnet sequence's heterosexual figurations—such as the unspecified "he" taking a bride in sonnet 3, drawing "the girls' attention" in 5, and wooing a feminized "Truth" in 6—as Auden passing for straight.

Although "Passenger Shanty" is omitted from the book, the Travel-Diary reflects the same anxiety that others might detect Auden and Isherwood's homosexuality. For example, their first appearance at a Hankow press conference draws "inquisitively hostile eyes" from the seasoned correspondents. Ostensibly, Auden and Isherwood feel out of place because they are journalist-poseurs—they confess that they "were not real journalists, but mere trippers"—yet the "hearty, square-shouldered, military-looking man" who acts as sentry alerts them, and the attentive reader, to the possible dangers of passing. Later on Auden and Isherwood encounter Dr. McClure at the American Mission Hospital; this "stalwart" Canadian Scot wears "a leather blouse, riding breeches and knee-boots with straps." Intimidated by McClure's "dynamic presence," Auden and Isherwood find themselves "uneasily suspecting" that he thinks them "slightly sissy." *Journey to a War*'s tightrope walk between covering and disclosing the authors' sexuality reflects the twofold dilemma Newton sees in the gay man's compulsory social performance: "First, he must conceal the fact that he sleeps with men. But concealing this *fact* is far less difficult than his second problem, which is controlling the *halo effect* or signals that would announce that he sleeps with men. The covert homosexual must in fact impersonate a *man*, that is, he must *appear* to the 'straight' world to be fulfilling (or not violating) all the requisites of the male role as defined by the 'straight' world."[21] Auden and Isherwood must rely on the straight male world of pressmen, doctors, missionaries, ambassadors, and military and government officials to aid their passage through China. To succeed in gathering the information necessary to their documentary book, they must first pass inspection.

Isherwood's omissions and codings also participate in the necessary drag of *Journey to a War*. *Christopher and His Kind* offers a direct rendering of Auden and Isherwood's erotic adventures when Isherwood recounts "afternoon holidays from their social consciences" in Shanghai. This posttext fills in *Journey to a War's* missing information about "a bathhouse where you were erotically soaped and massaged by young men." We also learn that "you could pick your attendants, and many of them were beautiful." Although *Christopher and His Kind* is quite open about these "pleasingly exotic" encounters, it echoes *Journey to a War's* anxieties about passing. Immediately after making his bathhouse disclosure, for example, Isherwood discusses his and Auden's act of concealing their sexual excursions from their Shanghai host, the British ambassador Sir Archibald Clark-Kerr: "Archie accepted their lies without comment, but a certain gleam in his eye made them wonder if he was playing a game with them." By contrast, the only mention of Shanghai bathhouses in *Journey to a War's* Travel-Diary divorces them from the authors' own experience and—more telling—frames them in the distancing, drag voice of "establishment" masculinity that characterizes British travel books: "Nevertheless the tired or lustful business man will find here everything to gratify his desires. You can buy an electric razor, or a French dinner, or a well-cut suit. . . . You can attend race-meetings, baseball games, football matches. You can see the latest American films. If you want girls, or boys, you can have them, at all prices, in the bathhouses and the brothels. If you want opium you can smoke it in the best company, served on a tray, like afternoon tea." Here the available "boys" are presented almost as an afterthought, sequestered by commas in a passage that otherwise presents the commodities "appropriate" to the well-traveled British businessman. The necessary drag of Isherwood's Travel-Diary even goes so far as to point out an incident at a train station in which a Chinese boy nudged him "in a sensitive place" and offered to procure a "'nice girl.'"[22]

Like its accounts of hostile eyes, the diary's account of Chinese boys allows the reader an occasional peek beneath the authors' drag costumes. Auden and Isherwood's stay at Journey's End—a mountain resort staffed by shorts-clad houseboys—is easily Journey to a War's most diversionary episode. Significantly, both Waugh and Plomer single out this episode as the book's high point; Plomer finds it one of the "two passages . . . where Mr. Isherwood gets a chance to be completely himself." Although these reviewers focus on the novelesque treatment of the hotel's eccentric proprietor (Mr. Charleton), the houseboys—whose "'beautiful legs'" he praises—give the episode much of its energy. In addition to the accommodating staff, each guest has, as Charleton puts it, "'a boy attached to him.'" Isherwood closes his account of Journey's End by describing the farewell tipping of the boys, who "giggled shamefacedly—as Europeans giggle over Sex—and asked for a little, a very little, just a trifle more."[23] Like Isherwood's remark about available Shanghai boys, this one linking boys, money, and sex serves as a textual wink at readers who can see through the authors' drag performance. Such "double-talk" opens a gap in Journey to a War, providing working space for Auden and Isherwood to call into question traditional masculinity. Their next strategy—camp—marks a transitional maneuver between concealing their own sexuality and critiquing the institution of Western male heterosexuality.

Whereas Fussell and Valentine Cunningham find the book's campiness inappropriate, I find it one of Journey to a War's most productive methods of confronting the politics of gender. Isherwood would go on to become one of the first commentators on camp in his 1956 novel The World in the Evening, so we should not be surprised to find its energies shaping his work of the late thirties. The necessary drag of passing can, according to Jack Babuscio, "lead to a heightened awareness and appreciation for disguise, impersonation, the projection of personality."[24] In Journey to a War, this theatrical aspect of camp is most apparent in Auden and Isherwood's self-representation, their second strategy of exposing the "front" of masculinity in documentary discourse. While their canon-breaking position as gay documentarists necessitates strategic camping, the elegant artifice they see in Chinese culture makes it easier.

To these English travelers, China blurs Western boundaries between the theatrical and the nontheatrical in ways similar to camp sensibility in gay culture. For example, the Travel-Diary devotes an entire entry to the Chinese opera *Lady Precious Stream,* a "highly artificial and ritualistic" affair with lavish robes and headpieces. The singers unsettle Western notions of stage boundaries by accepting tea from assistants after their more difficult songs—in full view of the audience. Gender boundaries also prove unstable at the opera; men perform the female roles with "faces transformed by make-up into pink and white masks." Edward Said asserts that such theatrical renderings of China replicate Orientalist constructions of the East "as spectacle, or *tableaux vivant,*" yet they also provide the gay writer a protective covering in which to present himself to his predominantly heterosexual audience. For example, the Travel-Diary costumes Isherwood in a "beret, sweater, and martial boots [that] would not be out of place in Valencia or Madrid"; he commented later in *Christopher and His Kind* that "Christopher was in masquerade as a war correspondent."[25]

Once *Journey to a War* establishes theatricality as a norm, Isherwood and Auden can stage their self-representation in ways that camp traditional masculinity while maintaining their pose as documentary men. The incongruous image of Isherwood in "Enemy planes overhead" camps conventional combat photography while capturing the surreality of the authors' search for the front (see fig. 27). *Journey to a War's* only photograph of Auden, captioned "In the trenches," pulls off its documentary posing with more success—but the attuned eye can still detect camp elements (fig. 28). Posing side by side with a Chinese soldier from the Grand Canal front, Auden appears on the scene of his reporterly duties. The soldier seems to cast Auden an admiring gaze beneath the brim of his cap, while the Englishman calmly regards the camera with a self-assured, close-lipped smile. Other soldiers, apparently unaware of the camera, go about their tasks in the background, further inflecting the photograph with documentary veracity. Yet the relation of background to foreground also gives this photograph a certain campiness—Auden's

28. "In the trenches," by W. H. Auden. From *Journey to a War.* (© by the Estate of W. H. Auden)

Western-cut, lighter-colored clothing and more brightly lit face make him appear out of place, as if he were matted into the shot. We return to his cryptic smile, which now seems to indicate his awareness of this discrepancy; he is *acting* the part of documentary man. Auden and Isherwood's drag performances push to a new level Peggy Phelan's recent contention that "all portrait photography is fundamentally performative."[26]

In the Travel-Diary, we often see the incongruity and humor of camp in accounts of the authors' train travel. For example, the Englishmen's presence on the Hankow-Chengchow train prompts many curious stares and smiles from the car boys, which prompts in turn a comical self-staging: "But perhaps we were not unimposing figures, with our superbly developed chests—padded out several inches by thick wads of Hankow dollar-bills stuffed into every available inner pocket." By humorously donning the big-chested disguise only to expose its artificiality, this self-representation deflates the authors and, more seriously, ridicules the he-man image of heterosexual masculinity. As Babuscio asserts, "Camp, by focusing on the outward appearances of role, implies that roles, and, in particular, sex roles, are superficial—a matter of style."[27] In Journey to a War's strategic camp, Auden and Isherwood don the garb of straight masculinity to challenge the equation of "straight" with "real."

Auden and Isherwood are not the only ones who perform masculinity in Journey to a War. Their extended portrait of Fleming serves as a third strategy of interrogating traditional masculinity; it too involves a theatrical understanding of maleness. In fact, Fleming upstages the authors whenever he enters the scene. They first encounter him with his wife, actress Celia Johnson, at a party in Hankow: "Fleming with his drawl, his tan, his sleek, perfectly brushed hair, and lean good looks, is a subtly comic figure—the conscious, living parody of the pukka sahib. He is altogether too good to be true—and he knows it." As it does throughout the Travel-Diary, Fleming's presence points up Auden and Isherwood's comparative lack of finesse while at the same time making his appearance of consummate manliness seem ridiculous—or, as Isherwood puts it, "almost absurdly correct." We can see this comic absurdity in Auden's photograph of Fleming, captioned "Special correspondent" (fig. 29). Clearly conscious of his performance, Fleming fingers his pipe and gazes off in pseudoreflection, all the while maintaining a flattering profile pose. Ironically, the "real" war reporter looks much less authentic here than Auden camping in the trenches. Fleming becomes the book's alpha male in the account of the southeastern front expedition—walking the entire distance, ca-

29. "Special correspondent (Peter Fleming)," by W. H. Auden. From *Journey to a War.* (© by the Estate of W. H. Auden)

joling troublesome traveling companions, negotiating with Chinese officials, typing dispatches while Auden and Isherwood sleep. And once again Fleming dresses for the part: "In his khaki shirt and shorts, complete with golf-stockings, strong suède shoes, water-proof wrist-watch and Leica camera, he might have stepped straight

from a London tailor's window, advertising Gent's Tropical Explo-
ration Kit."[28] "Straight" indeed, this well-groomed, heterosexual
Etonian typifies his culture's preferred model of the globe-trotting
Englishman.

By calling attention to this straight man's performing body in the
camp context of *Journey to a War,* Auden and Isherwood anticipate
Butler's performative theory of gender, in which "the parodic replication
and resignification of heterosexual constructs within non-heterosexual
frames brings into relief the utterly constructed status of the so-
called original." In fact, one could argue that Auden and Isherwood
prompt a more radical rethinking of gender because drag—Butler's
prime example of "heterosexual constructs" in gay and lesbian contexts—is also performed through heterosexual bodies. By showing
that the heterosexual Fleming is just as theatrical in his resourceful
masculinity as they are in their documentary drag, Auden and Isherwood also reveal the same "inevitable exchange of meanings in the
prefixes 'homo' and 'hetero'" that Edelman finds in the practice of
"homographesis"—a productive tension in which compulsory heterosexuality is written and unwritten or, to use Edelman's terms, "*in*-
scribed" and "*de*-scribed." Auden and Isherwood employ this dynamic by presenting Fleming as the alpha male they fall short of *and*
as the "absurdly correct" figure they can see through. A "double operation," homographesis both codifies and resists "the ideological
purposes of a conservative social order"; it provides the gay writer
with a means of subverting the dominant culture from within its dis-
ciplinary frameworks.[29]

Once *Journey to a War* begins the work of unwriting Western masculinity, it clears a space in which to rewrite it—a project Auden
takes on in the commentary to *In Time of War.* This fourth strategy of
interrogating masculinity critiques the "great men" of civilization, revealing dominant accounts of the past as both oppressive and aggressively male. Again, China's unsettling of Western gender roles provides a conducive environment for Auden to interrogate masculinity;
the Travel-Diary cautions that Western impressions of "Chinese military morale" are inevitably superficial because "in Europe one is so
accustomed to cocksureness and boasting that the reticence of a Chinese officer seems positively defeatist."[30] Just as H.D. would decenter

patriarchal mythologies in *Trilogy* (her response to World War II), Auden here decenters history's conquering "hero" by bringing gender to bear on the violence that drives civilization.

Auden's commentary contextualizes the late thirties as "the epoch of the Third Great Disappointment," following the trigger points of the Roman Empire and the Reformation. Bringing together West and East, Auden links the historical march of male tyrants to the current crisis of fascism—represented as the "inhuman and triumphant" voice that bids the world to "Leave Truth to the police and us." Then he stages the "great men" of history joining the fascist rally to voice their approval:

> All the great conquerors sit upon their platform,
> Lending their sombre weight of practical experience:
> *Ch'in Shih Huang Ti* who burnt the scholars' books,
>
> *Chaka* the mad who segregated the two sexes,
> And *Genghis Khan* who thought mankind should be destroyed,
> And *Diocletian* the administrator make impassioned speeches.
>
> *Napoleon* claps who found religion useful,
> And all who passed deception of the People, or who said
> Like Little *Frederick*, "I shall see that it is done."

This is hardly laudatory—these swaggering figures make others pay the price for their aggressive male posturing and conquest narratives. Backed by the thinking of Plato, Machiavelli, Hobbes, and other influential men who shape Western history—Auden terms them "famous clerks" supporting the "programme"—the conquerors set in motion a destructive cycle that contemporary world leaders repeat anew:

> Nor do our leaders help; we know them now
> For humbugs full of vain dexterity, invoking
> A gallery of ancestors . . .

Heads of state during this buildup to World War II were, of course, all men. The commentary of *In Time of War* genders "the West's barnstorming threadbare individual" that Stan Smith sees as Auden's primary target, revealing that the sonnet sequence's unspecified uses of "he" do not, as Herbert Greenberg argues, refer simply to "*Man* the species." Sonnet 13—which O'Neill and Reeves find central to understanding the sequence—prefigures Auden's antipatriarchal history lesson, acknowledging ironically that while "there have been great men," their achievements cannot undo "the morning's injured weeping," or the fact that "all princes must / Employ the Fairly-Noble unifying Lie" that eventually breeds fascism.[31] I would not call Auden's critique of patriarchal history in *In Time of War* a feminist one. As with thirties documentary films, women are usually out of the picture; they appear infrequently as shadowy figures of speech, as passive wives (sonnet 2), as dominating mothers (sonnet 5). Yet because Auden too is positioned at the margins of a patriarchal culture, he attacks the ideology of "great men" in ways that sometimes intersect with critiques such as Virginia Woolf's *Three Guineas*, which lambastes the institution of biography for excluding women.

In contrast to modern-day fascists and the dictators who preceded them, Auden presents an anonymous, ungendered collective—"the Invisible College of the Humble"—in the commentary's closing pages. These are the "others," he asserts, "Who through all the ages have accomplished everything essential." As sonnet 24 insists,

No, not their [great men's] names. It was the others who built
Each great coercive avenue and square,
Where men can only recollect and stare,
The really lonely with the sense of guilt

Who wanted to persist like that for ever;
The unloved had to leave material traces:
But these need nothing but our better faces . . .

In other words, it is the unheroic, unconquering masses who really effect progress and establish justice, not the great men who erect vainglorious monuments to themselves and control the dominant version of history. As Smith asserts, Auden's Invisible College "is not just a collectivity, but a place of learning and teaching"; in it we learn to form coalitions that counter the violence of patriarchy.[32]

In the self-reflective text of *Journey to a War*, Auden and Isherwood scrutinize their own culture, revealing the ways that gender politics—specifically, Western constructions of masculinity—distort their "firsthand experience" of China. Recently, Joseph A. Boone has shown that for male French and British writers, Egypt and the Near East "put into crisis assumptions about male sexual desire, masculinity, and heterosexuality that are specific to Western culture"—the same dynamic that Auden and Isherwood confronted in China. It is impossible for them—or any European male traveler—to enter the East without preconceptions of what they will see. The sestet to Auden's hybrid sonnet "The Ship" acknowledges this inevitable mediation:

> It is our culture that with such calm progresses
> Over the barren plains of a sea; somewhere ahead
> The Septic East, a war, new flowers and new dresses.
>
> Somewhere a strange and shrewd To-morrow goes to bed
> Planning the test for men from Europe; no one guesses
> Who will be most ashamed, who richer, and who dead.[33]

The word "progresses," which introduces feminine rhyme to the poem, is surely ironic, for not only is the Westerners' route "barren," but it also leads to a destination that will prove pathogenic to their ideology. Focusing specifically on "*men* from Europe," Auden invokes Isherwood's idea of "The Test" for thirties men too young to have proved their manhood in World War I. The gnawing question "'Are you really a Man'" now governs the travelers' voyage to the East, which becomes a testing ground that challenges the English authors' understanding of masculinity in three ways. First, the Sino-Japanese War becomes a last chance for them to at least see the front, if not fight there. In addition, China unsettles Western masculinity by prompting Auden and Isherwood to stage it in "new dresses." Finally, the East bears signs of European imperialist conquest, signs that also mark the passages of earlier exploring men. We see this quite clearly in the book's map—which shows European colonies such as British Hong Kong, Portuguese Macao, and French Indochina—and in the diary's account of Western missions that host the English travelers. Intersecting with the conquest narratives of Western patriarchy, imperialism shaped thirties documentary discourse in ways that worked against its aims to reveal "other" cultures' reality and to advocate on "their" behalf.

Negotiating Imperialism in *Journey to a War*

In his commentary to *In Time of War,* Auden refers to the authors "Casting our European shadows on Shanghai"; this line acknowledges that, as Said puts it, a Westerner "comes up against the Orient as a European or American first, as an individual second." Surprisingly, few reviewers and critics of *Journey to a War* have questioned their documentary expectations by considering Britain's imperialist relation to China—and British documentary film's own imperialist genealogy. Two notable exceptions are Kirstein and Smith. Kirstein declared the book's primary subject to be "the conscience of a Western ruling class faced with the agony of an Oriental people to whom they feel responsibility"; yet his contemporary review, like Smith's later Auden study, failed to consider how *Journey to a War* is also complicit in imperialist vision. Swingler's complaint that Auden and Isherwood "are helplessly lost in the struggle of modern China" shows a more typical investment in the eyewitness authority that fueled thirties documentary. But in assuming that two Englishmen can "find out what is really happening" in China, Swingler completely ignored Europe's history of colonizing the East.[34]

He had only to read the Travel-Diary's opening pages to see how Western financial interests controlled access to "modern China"— even for the Japanese. This fact was certainly not lost on Auden and Isherwood as they sailed from Hong Kong—which would become one of Britain's longest-held colonies—to Canton and their first contact with Chinese soil: "Warehouses began to crowd along the banks; many of them had Union Jacks, swastikas, or Stars and Stripes painted upon their roofs. We imagined a comic drawing of a conscientious Japanese observer looking down in perplexity from a bombing-plane upon a wilderness of neutral flags, and finally espying a tiny, unprotected Chinese patch: 'Don't you think,' he says, 'we might be able to fit a little one in, just there?'" If an Asian might find China difficult to locate beneath the "front" of Western imperialism, then British observers would certainly find it so. In his account of *Journey to a War,* Hynes has argued that Swingler based his expectation "on the experience of Spain" and failed to consider what distinguished the Sino-Japanese War from the Spanish Civil War.[35] Hynes locates the key difference in the larger-scale destruction in China, but we must also consider the Englishmen's conflicted cultural position toward Asia.

On the one hand, invaded China became another link in the United Front against fascism, prompting support from Western leftist coalitions in ways similar to Republican Spain, though to a lesser degree. The Communist Eighth Route Army in particular drew a number of leftist observers, including Capa, Ferno, Joris Ivens, and the American activist Agnes Smedley. Germany, Italy, and Japan's emerging configuration as World War II's Axis powers also placed China on the "us" side of the equation. Auden and Isherwood's dispatch for *New Masses*, "Meeting the Japanese," reflects an *alliance* between English observer and Chinese observed by opening with bold advocacy: "For us, in Canton, in Hankow, along the Yellow River, the Japanese were 'the enemy'; the Chinese anti-aircraft were 'our' guns, the Chinese planes 'our' planes, the Chinese army was 'we.'"[36]

On the other hand, a deeper configuration underlies this one and contradicts it. The East's historical position as the site of both Europe's colonies and its "other" places England and China on opposite sides, invoking what Said calls the Orientalist "vision of reality whose structure promoted the difference between the familiar (Europe, the West, 'us') and the strange (the Orient, the East, 'them')." Auden and Isherwood's travelogue for *Harpers Bazaar*, "Escales," reflects this *opposition* between European observer and Asian observed by describing Singhalese natives "jostl[ing] aimlessly down ramshackle lanes of shops crammed with all the gaudy, eye-catching trash of the East."[37] Regarding Ceylon with what Mary Louise Pratt calls the "imperial eyes" of European explorers and travelers, the English writers inherit a way of seeing that works against their advocacy for any Asian country—even one that has fallen prey to bombing raids. The divergent accounts of the East in "Meeting the Japanese" and "Escales" anticipate the incompatible visions of China that trouble *Journey to a War.*

Returning British documentary practice to the site of empire, the book both coincides and collides with imperialist vision in ways that trigger the genre's deconstruction. Orientalist perceptions of the East often thwart attempts to engage with wartime China; the two Englishmen will inevitably cast their "European shadows on Shanghai." But as the ambiguity of Auden's word *casting* suggests, their position in China is a riddled one. Casting shadows can mean at least three things in *Journey to a War:* Auden and Isherwood confer their own culture's interpretive framework on what they encounter; they assign roles to the European presence in Asia; and they drop their culture's interpretive framework in order to see China differently. These multiple responses support Lisa Lowe's recent contention that "Orientalism is irregularly composed of statements and restatements, contestations, and accommodations, generated from an incongruous series of writing positions" that are freighted with gender and sexuality as well as with class, race, and nation. Moreover, *Journey to a War's* status as a gay text unsettles the structural similarity Lowe sees between "the occidental fascination with the Orient and the male lover's passion for his female beloved"—the same heterosexual framework that Boone faults in Said's *Orientalism.*[38] If we return for a moment to Isherwood's camp description of the authors' money-padded shirts, we can see that the semblance of "superbly developed chests" reflects both Auden and Isherwood's outsider position among documentary men *and* their empowered position as affluent European males in an Eastern country. Such theatrical negotiations with the East in *Journey to a War* precipitate shifts between the first and third meanings of European shadow casting. A triptych of representations from the Travel-Diary, the poems, and the Picture Commentary illustrates these shifting positions toward China.

In some parts of the book, Auden and Isherwood impose European frameworks on China and her people. Theatrical tropes in these passages position the authors as Orientalist observers who script the East with the imperial narratives of British culture. For example, an early passage in the Travel-Diary records their first meeting with the governor of Kwantung Province (General Wu Teh-chen), an encounter that fails to meet his English visitors' highly choreographed expectations:

> We began to move into the dining-room, still talking; there seemed to be no special order of precedence. All this informality, admirable as it was, disappointed us a little. Both Auden and myself were still steeped in the traditions of *The Chinese Bungalow.* We had even rehearsed the scene beforehand, and prepared *suitable* compliments and speeches. The Governor *should have said,* "My poor house is honoured." And we should have replied: "Our feet are quite unworthy to rest upon your

honourable doorstep." On which, the Governor, *had he known his stuff,* would have cracked back: "If my doorstep were gold, it would hardly be fit for your distinguished shoes." And so on. Perhaps, after all, it was a good thing that General Wu was unacquainted with the subtleties of European stage-Chinese, or we might never have reached the lunch-table.

Despite the account's satirical humor and irony, Auden and Isherwood follow Orientalist practice in having Europe determine what is "suitably" Asian. Isherwood may engage in occasional self-deprecation by confessing the ridiculousness of their assumptions, yet he nonetheless frames the meeting with General Wu as a disappointment. Moreover, the Travel-Diary shores up the Englishmen's expectations by citing a prior Orientalist text, a play that billed itself as "a melodrama of the Far East." Performed on the London stage in 1929, *The Chinese Bungalow* revolved around an unhappily married English woman, her wealthy Chinese husband, and an available English planter; the actor who played the husband drew a nod from the *Times* for dying "with *appropriate* consideration for his ancestral honour." By citing *The Chinese Bungalow,* the Travel-Diary eschews China and engages in Orientalism's self-referential practice that Lowe calls "cultural quotation."[39]

Isherwood, in fact, predicts the endurance of such "romantic and false" images toward the end of the diary, when he constructs a panorama of the Chinese landscape through the "picture-frame" of a ship's porthole:

The brown river in the rain, the boatmen in their dark bat-wing capes, the tree-crowned pagodas on the foreshore, the mountains scarved in mist—these were no longer features of the beautiful, prosaic country we had just left behind us; they were the scenery of the traveler's dream; they were the mysterious, *l'Extrême Orient.* Memory in the years to come would prefer this simple theatrical picture to all the subtle and chaotic impressions of the past months. This, I thought— despite all we have seen, heard, experienced—is how I shall finally remember China.

Here Isherwood's allusions to pictures and frames intersect with the painterly discourse that Pratt finds in the "monarch-of-all-I-survey genre" of Victorian male travel writing. "If the scene is a painting," Pratt argues in her analysis of Richard Burton's *Lake Regions of Central*

Africa, the explorer "is both the viewer there to judge and appreciate it, and the verbal painter who produces it for others." Like Burton, Isherwood "discovers" his own preconceptions about an "other" country and takes possession of it, though as a self-conscious stage manager instead of a masterful explorer. The theatrical discourse of "scenery" allows a more active, populated landscape than the static vistas Pratt assesses, but the natives' movements can only follow the European director's choreography.[40]

Other parts of *Journey to a War* employ the second sense of "casting shadows" by assigning roles to the Europeans Auden and Isherwood encounter on their journey to the East. This way of seeing is somewhat similar to the strategy of exposing the observer in *Letters from Iceland,* but the larger political implications of Europe's imperial presence in Asia reveal a deeper, more cultural complicity in the unequal relations between observer and observed. Again the East is figured in terms of theater, but this time it is Westerners who perform on the imperial stage. Auden's opening poem "Hongkong," which serves as the authors' entry point to China and the reader's entry point to the Travel-Diary, marks *Journey to a War*'s most extended use of theatrical tropes:

> The leading characters are wise and witty;
> Substantial men of birth and education
> With wide experience of administration,
> They know the manners of a modern city.
>
> Only the servants enter unexpected;
> Their silence has a fresh dramatic use:
> Here in the East the bankers have erected
> A worthy temple to the Comic Muse.
>
> Ten thousand miles from home and What's-her-name,
> The bugle on the Late Victorian hill
> Puts out the soldier's light; off-stage, a war
>
> Thuds like the slamming of a distant door:
> We cannot postulate a General Will;
> For what we are, we have ourselves to blame.

Rich with undercutting feminine rhyme, this satirical poem establishes a countertheater to the Orientalist melodrama of *The Chinese*

Bungalow. All the coordinates of British power—class ("birth and education"), masculinity ("erected"), heterosexuality ("What's-her-name"),
and imperial conquest ("the Late Victorian hill")—place the "leading
characters" at the center of the Eastern stage. But as Smith points
out, "the theatricality of their self-importance is farcical" because
"the plot actually belongs to those they regard as minor parts."[41] The
delayed turn in this hybrid sonnet shows that the Sino-Japanese War
is an "off-stage" event for the British financiers who view the East
solely in terms of economic gain. With a shock of recognition, the
"we" of the closing lines marks the authors' complicity with their English culture, thus making possible their shifts from conferring to
dropping imperialist perceptions in *Journey to a War.*

Auden and Isherwood do, on occasion, wrench themselves from
their culture's interpretive framework so that they can see China in
non-Orientalist ways. The most striking examples occur when figurations of China as "us" and "them" intersect. In such textual moments, they see China as a *doubly occupied* country, suffering inva-
sions by the Japanese army and by an expansionist Western economy.
This double vision certainly informs Auden's photograph "Japanese
sentry," which appears in the "Soldiers and Civilians" section of the
Picture Commentary (fig. 30). Initially, Auden's juxtaposition of the
rigid Japanese soldier with the "Drink Watson's" billboard appears to
be an amused appreciation of visual incongruity. But are these signs
that compete for the viewer's attention really unrelated? By showing
another "tiny, unprotected Chinese patch" of ground caught between
Japanese firepower and British economic power, the photograph
questions the authors'—and their country's—claim to side with China
in this war.

A similar recognition occurs in the book's account of a lunch
meeting with Japanese civilians at the Shanghai Club, arranged by "a
prominent British business man." As the Japanese men justify their
country's occupation of China, Isherwood looks out the window and
sees another occupier, one of the gunboats that protect British-owned
ships: "At this moment, through the dining-room window which
overlooked the river, the gun-turrets of H.M.S. *Birmingham* slid qui-
etly into view, moving upstream. In this city the visual statements of
power-politics are more brutal than any words." Like the English ad-
vertisement in Auden's photograph, the British gunboat in Isherwood's description becomes the out-of-place element in China; such

30. "Japanese sentry," by W. H. Auden. From *Journey to a War.* (© by the Estate of W. H. Auden)

critiques of Britain's imperial presence in the East contest the Orientalist descriptions that also appear in *Journey to a War.* These incompatible positions toward China wrestle with one another, distorting the travelers' documentary scrutiny and confronting the genre with its imperialist origins. Caught between shifting fronts, Auden and Isherwood find themselves in the same quandary that Susan Sontag would describe decades later in postwar China: "But to continue the trip, neither colonialist nor native, is an ingenious task."[42] As their vantage points for viewing Hankow air raids make clear—the towering rooftop of the American Bank, the manicured lawn of the British consulate—imperial vision will inevitably impose itself between the Western authors and the Sino-Japanese War.

Documentary Dilemmas

Documentary vision in *Journey to a War* comes to a crisis in Japanese-occupied Shanghai, where Auden and Isherwood conscientiously seek out exploited workers, wounded soldiers, and homeless refugees to record for their Western audience. Yet their Shanghai lodging (the British ambassador's villa, Number One House) becomes another "visual statement of power-politics" that marks the authors' unbridgeable distance from those they observe. In the closing paragraphs of the Travel-Diary, Isherwood invokes this separation to question the value of their documentary enterprise: "And we ourselves though we wear out our shoes walking the slums, though we take notes, though we are genuinely shocked and indignant, belong, unescapably, to the other world. We return, always, to Number One House for lunch."[43] The Travel-Diary ends with paralysis as Isherwood confesses the authors' inability to change—or even understand—the miseries they encounter.

Auden's commentary presents a more conflicted response to the authors' estrangement from wartime China:

> While in an international and undamaged quarter,
> Casting our European shadows on Shanghai,
> Walking unhurt among the banks, apparently immune
>
> Below the monuments of an acquisitive society,
> With friends and books and money and the traveller's freedom,
> We are compelled to realize that our refuge is a sham.

In the context of the commentary's antifascist message, the protection afforded by "European shadows" proves to be a "sham" because the Sino-Japanese War becomes a "local variant" of approaching global crisis.[44] But the documentary context of *Journey to a War* contradicts this meaning—and concurs with Isherwood—by disconnecting Western observer and Eastern observed. Instead of shedding light on what they observe, Auden and Isherwood *cast their shadows* on it;

their representations mark their privileged position and thus expose documentary's claims of advocacy as a "sham." Such moments of disconcerting self-reflectiveness enable *Journey to a War* to offer a critique from within thirties documentary practice.

Three photographs from the Picture Commentary further this interrogation from within by exposing the observers' unequal power. Representing the poor, a staple subject of documentary discourse, this triptych of images depicts a beggar at Lung-Hai Railway Station and refugees in Shanghai.[45] In the first two images Auden casts shadows by including in the frame the observers' mode of transport to the scene. Shot from either a train window or a station platform, the photograph captioned "Train parasites" shows an elderly person holding a basket up toward Auden; rigid lines of the train track intrude on the center of the frame (fig. 31). The beggar's abject expression and missing teeth render him or her as documentary's typical object of pity. Yet the image also troubles the genre by making visible the contrasts between observer and observed—the mobile, downward-looking photographer scrutinizes an immobile beggar whose eyes are closed.

"Refugees in camp," the second image in this triptych, also unsettles documentary by recording barriers between observer and observed; here the Shanghai refugees are literally marked off from the outside world by the foregrounded, diagonal curb (fig. 32). In stark contrast to their hovels made of scrap material is the sleek automobile at the frame's left edge, probably the car Auden and Isherwood used to reach the refugee camp. If *Journey to a War* were a more polished documentary text, this touristic feature would be cropped out—yet the car's inclusion is what makes its critique of "the traveller's freedom" possible. Unlike the man who squares his shoulders toward the camera at the frame's right edge, Auden is free to observe these people, photograph them, and move on. Auden's images of Chinese refugees record documentary's imperialism by reminding us that, in Said's words, "a certain freedom of intercourse was always the Westerner's privilege; because his was the stronger culture, he could penetrate."[46]

We see an even more disturbing example of documentary penetration in the third photograph, "La condition humaine," which shows the interior of a refugees' dwelling (fig. 33). In this snapshot, two

31. "Train parasites," by W. H. Auden. From *Journey to a War.* (© by the Estate of W. H. Auden)

weary-looking men and a boy gather around a makeshift dinner table; the foremost man looks resentfully over his shoulder at Auden's intrusion. Adding to this visual disturbance is the trace of Isherwood's body along the frame's left edge, which marks the viewer's complicity in documentary's class voyeurism. More than any other representation in *Journey to a War,* this image exposes the politics of representing human suffering in an Eastern country.

Auden's ambiguously allusive caption—"La condition humaine"— departs from those of the first two photographs by connecting the Sino-Japanese War to other events and persons that shaped leftist documentary discourse in the 1930s. Because of this larger domain, the caption and image become Auden's ironic commentary on his growing estrangement from the decade's documentary men. *La condition humaine* (1933), the historical novel that established André

32. "Refugees in camp," by W. H. Auden. From *Journey to a War.* (© by the Estate of W. H. Auden)

Malraux's international reputation, recounts Shanghai's failed communist uprising of 1927 from the perspective of its collective protagonist, three revolutionaries. (Auden met and photographed two leaders who were on opposite sides of this conflict—Chou En-lai and Du Yueh-seng.) Born six years before Auden, Malraux was considered one of the "committed" artists of his generation and an unwavering fellow traveler with communists. Auden had written in *The Poet's Tongue* that the business of poetry was "making the necessity for action more urgent and its nature more clear," but Malraux had been taking action. In 1936 he flew with an international air squadron to fight for Republican Spain, thus lending to his pro-Republican novel (*L'espoir*) more credibility than Auden's radio broadcasting did to *Spain.* If anyone could provide "authentic" accounts of thirties crises, most leftists believed, it was Malraux. But unlike Auden, Malraux never set foot in Shanghai until *after* his representations of that city were published. In fact, Mary M. Rowan contends that Malraux's obscured rendering of Shanghai proves "important only as a stage set-

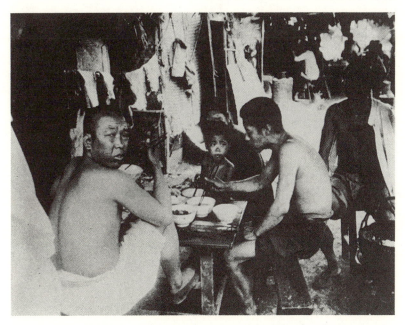

33. "La condition humaine," by W. H. Auden. From *Journey to a War.* (© by the Estate of W. H. Auden)

ting for revolution." So while Auden's photograph may concur with Malraux by implying that Shanghai would have been better served by the communist revolutionaries, it also contends with him by countering the novelist's revolutionary heroes with documentary images of displaced refugees that detail their squalid environment. Auden's photograph also critiques its own making—and with it John Grierson's 1937 claim that documentary representation can "sen[se] the *condition humaine* across the distance of nationality."[47] Riddled with contradictions like the larger collaborative text that contains them, Auden's text and image reach documentary impasse.

Lucy McDiarmid has written that Auden and Isherwood's collaborative plays reject artistic models that "assum[e] a colonialistic authority over" human subjects, thus reflecting the authors' "greater confidence in disestablishing than in establishing (or asserting) authority."[48] If "colonialistic authority" is at stake in the plays, which McDiarmid links to Auden's work with documentary films, then it is certainly more so in *Journey to a War*—a documentary travelogue whose production placed the English writers at the site of Europe's Eastern empires. In fact, we can read this text as British documentary film's metaphoric return to its imperialist origins in the Empire Marketing Board. Grierson's E.M.B. Film Unit preceded Auden and Isherwood's eastward journey through British colonies with *Song of Ceylon* (1934), sponsored by the Ceylon Tea Propaganda Board. Although director Basil Wright circumvented the sponsor by showing the intrusion of Britain's tea industry on native life, the film commentary's uninterrogated use of a seventeenth-century explorer's narrative positions this documentary production within the history of empire.

The commentary to Auden's sonnet sequence, which ends *Journey to a War,* certainly invites comparisons to his commentaries for the E.M.B. Film Unit's successor, the G.P.O. Film Unit. Echoing the closing sequence of *Night Mail* in which a repressive sleep settles over Glasgow, Edinburgh, and Aberdeen, this commentary's closing sequence cloaks its domain in darkness:

> Night falls on China; the great arc of travelling shadow
> Moves over land and ocean, altering life:
> Thibet already silent, the packed Indias cooling,
>
> Inert in the paralysis of caste. And though in Africa
> The vegetation still grows fiercely like the young,
> And in the cities that receive the slanting radiations
>
> The lucky are at work, and most still know they suffer,
> The dark will touch them soon:

Significantly, it is a colonial geography—Asia and Africa—that falls under this life-altering "shadow"; by contrast the European cities, which receive "slanting radiations," have not yet succumbed to darkness. The connection between Auden's commentary and the *Night Mail* verse becomes clearer if we return to the latter the expunged lines linking colonialism to industrial Britain, documentary's focal point of the early 1930s. Previously, the poem had included textile towns in the mail train's itinerary: "In grimed Dundee that weaves a white linen from / the Indian fibre, in Stornoway smoking its heavy wools."[49] Auden's play with darkness and light not only invokes the chiaroscuro of thirties documentary images, but also comments ironically on how an imperialist economy soils Britain's textile industry.

Curiously, no account survives as to why these lines disappeared from the verse commentary. In an interview with Elizabeth Sussex, Wright recalls Auden's tendency "to make verbal images which were too violent for the pictorial content," citing as an example his description of the Cheviots as "uplands heaped like slaughtered horses."[50] Yet this rationale would hardly explain the omission of Dundee and Stornoway from a portion of the film that depicts several industrial scenes. Although Auden's troubling lines were stricken from *Night Mail*, documentary's links to imperialism would return to vex his and Isherwood's self-conscious encounters with China and the East in *Journey to a War*. Auden's final documentary text of the thirties forces an extended confrontation between British documentary practice and its imperialist genealogy, effecting a deconstruction of the genre.

As this chapter has shown, the poems, prose, and photographs of *Journey to a War* pressure documentary representation along two fault lines: the heterosexual/homosexual binarism that defines Western constructions of masculinity, and the colonizer/colonized binarism that underpins the Griersonian model of British documentary. By revealing the dominant perspective of thirties documentary as that of the heterosexual imperial male, Auden and Isherwood expose as a front the genre's pretense of giving voice to the "other" people it represents—whether Eastern colonials or British workers. Consider, for example, the patriotic, nation-claiming voice that closes the film *Industrial Britain:* "We build materials for power [shot of dynamos]. We build materials for transport [shots of a train, a truck]. We build colossal road trains for India and West Africa to go where no roadway can be built [shots of a vehicle with oversized tires]. These are the products of industrial Britain [shots of a worker's torso, a worker's forearms over a shovel]." Incorporating Asia and Africa into its imperial "we," the film unintentionally exposes its own imperialist vision, prompting the viewer to see its objectified images of coal miners and steelworkers as the colonial within, as "material" in the service of empire. The genealogy of this vision includes not only *Industrial Britain's* sponsor, the Empire Marketing Board, but British nationalism itself. Discussing documentary's appeal to thirties British writers, Cunningham remarks, "Documentary film was Ours, it was British."[51] For the Auden of *Journey to a War*, documentary's "Britishness" proved to be one of its greatest inadequacies.

Documentary's metaphoric return to empire in *Journey to a War* prompts us to examine more closely Grierson's characterization of the British documentary film movement in the 1930s. The rhetoric of male imperial conquest erupts sporadically in his publications justifying "the documentary men's" goals and defending them from their detractors. In "The Course of Realism" he describes documentary films as ground-staking "flags of vitality . . . flown over the British cinemas." Grierson's most blatantly imperialist defense of documentary filmmaking also occurs in this essay: "We have taken our cameras to the more difficult *territory*. We have set up our tripods among the *Yahoos* themselves, and schools have gathered round us." Giving his documentary men the conquering vision of imperial eyes, Grierson likens them to swaggering explorers who conquer "hostile" countries by "attack[ing] new materials and bring[ing] them into visual focus on the screen."[52] To what extent can documentary bear effective witness to some social inequalities while participating in others? For Auden, a gay man writing and photographing against the grain of dominant documentary practice, this contradiction became insurmountable by the end of the thirties.

6

AFTERWORD

"I Am Not a Camera"

NOT LONG after his travels through war-torn China, Auden emigrated to New York and continued responding to the global conflicts that were converging into World War II. But he rejected the documentary strategies he had adapted with such mixed feelings in the thirties. John Grierson's bold statements about documentary men waging a "battle for authenticity" rang hollow for the disillusioned Auden who contemplated an embattled world in "September 1, 1939":

> I sit in one of the dives
> On Fifty-Second Street
> Uncertain and afraid
> As the clever hopes expire
> Of a low dishonest decade:
> Waves of anger and fear
> Circulate over the bright
> And darkened lands of the earth,
> Obsessing our private lives;
> The unmentionable odour of death
> Offends the September night.[1]

Radio propaganda—"waves of anger and fear"—now eclipsed the artistic interventions that had warned of the consequences of class inequality and fascism. The Western democracies' failure to fight Hitler and Mussolini in Spain had ensured the Republic's defeat. Britain's government had appeased Hitler's fascist regime, which now threatened more of Europe—and Britain itself. As the 1930s spiraled toward their catastrophic ending, many in the Auden generation questioned the value of their earlier efforts to enlist art toward progressive social change.

171

Auden reached his own trigger point at the end of the decade that brought his writing and documentary representation to prominence. Like many leftist writers who came of age in the thirties, Auden had believed that this new form could provide a more engaged and effective stance toward a crisis-ridden world. Carrying cameras—or using them figuratively in their writing—documentary observers sought to establish contact across class and national boundaries. Their presence at coal mines, factories, slums, war fronts, and refugee camps attested to their genuine desire to understand and intervene in the social problems of their day. Yet the documentary movements that triggered these touristic excursions into others' lives were often blind to the imperial male politics of their own representations. As Auden interacted with documentary through film, photography, and literature, he came to believe that the genre could no longer withstand the external pressures of world events and the internal pressures of its own contradictions.

After *Journey to a War* Auden separated his writing from documentary representation, abandoning photo-textual collaborations and eyewitness accounts for his more abstract ruminations of the 1940s. Although he traveled to Germany to interview civilians for the U.S. Strategic Bombing Survey in 1945, Auden declined the opportunity to coauthor a book about his and James Stern's observations. In this decade he produced his tour de force poems *For the Time Being* (an updated oratorio of the Nativity story), *The Sea and the Mirror* (an interaction with Shakespeare's *The Tempest*), and *The Age of Anxiety* (a Jungian diagnosis of the modern psyche). This shift in literary style was not a shift from social consciousness, but an effort to create new artistic forms in the face of World War II and its aftermath.

Auden continued to interrogate the politics of representation in his post-1930s career. In the essay "Squares and Oblongs" (1948), for example, he reconsiders poetry's capacity to represent—in both senses of the word—catastrophic human suffering:

> There are events which arouse such simple and obvious emotions that an AP cable or a photograph in *Life* magazine are enough and poetic comment is impossible. If one reads through the mass of versified trash inspired, for instance, by the Lidice Massacre, one cannot avoid the conclusion that what was really bothering the versifiers was a feel-

ing of guilt at not feeling horrorstruck enough. Could a good poem have been written on such a subject? Possibly. One that revealed this lack of feeling, that told how when he read the news, the poet, like you and I, dear reader, went on thinking about his fame or his lunch, and how glad he was that he was not one of the victims.[2]

As happened with Guernica, Hitler's 1942 destruction of the Czech village of Lidice prompted many literary responses that drew images from photojournalism and newsreels. But Auden now departed from thirties writers' tendency to emulate and compete with documentary forms when representing the destruction of human lives. Instead of opening new possibilities for socially engaged literature, he pronounces, the arresting images of war reportage and atrocity photographs close down "poetic comment." Or do they? "Squares and Oblongs" may concede the scenes of war's atrocities to photojournalism, but it reserves for poetry the role of critiquing the resulting images' production and consumption.

In proposing a poetic response to the Lidice massacre that depicts the artist and audience instead of the victims they observe, Auden calls into question his culture's dominant models of representing social crisis. Photojournalism and documentary claim to bridge the distance between viewer and victims by eliciting sympathy, but Auden contends that the opposite is true. Acknowledging his own complicity in the voyeurism and self-centeredness that drive our compulsion to view others' suffering, he reveals newspaper readers' inability to connect images of the Lidice victims with their daily life. In a society that was already becoming desensitized to representations of atrocities, Auden decides that war poetry can best achieve social efficacy by offering counterreadings of the images we rely on to apprehend the violence of our century. As he wrote in "Memorial for the City"—his only publication evoking his experiences with the Bombing Survey—"The steady eyes of the crow and the camera's candid eye / See as honestly as they know how, but they lie."[3]

Auden also interrogated his generation's dominant models of socially engaged art at the end of the 1960s, another decade of widespread social unrest. A new generation of leftist artists and intellectuals sought strategies for intervening in a troubled world, and they often drew their models from the 1930s. In America, James Agee and Walker Evans's *Let Us Now Praise Famous Men* was finding renewed social relevance among civil rights activists in the South. *Authors Take Sides on Vietnam* echoed its predecessor *Authors Take Sides on the Spanish War,* and Auden was once again called on to issue a statement. This time he used the occasion to question the value of enlisting writers to comment on political issues, declaring that "their views have no more authority than those of any reasonably well-educated citizen." He also pointed to the cultural divide that rendered problematic Western observations of the Vietnamese conflict: "But what do I, or any other writer in the West, know about Vietnam, except what we can glean from the newspapers and a few hurriedly written books?"[4] In other words, Auden reminded his fellow writers of the need to acknowledge the imperial frameworks that mediate their understanding of Asian countries—a lesson he had learned through his attempts to gain access to the Sino-Japanese War. As he did in the thirties, Auden asks socially engaged artists to examine the assumptions behind their practice.

In the aphoristic poem "I Am Not a Camera," written in 1969, Auden revisits the documentary decade in which he came of age and contests its reliance on photographic vision. The title counters Christopher Isherwood's literary impersonation of a camera in *Goodbye to Berlin:* "I am a camera with its shutter open, quite passive, recording, not thinking. Recording the man shaving at the window opposite and the woman in the kimono washing her hair." Although Isherwood blended fact and fiction in his autobiographical stories and novels, his contemporaries and subsequent critics have often used these lines to discuss the veracity that documentary film and photography supposedly lend to writing. Yet such characterizations fail to examine realist assumptions about photographic representation: that the physical world presents itself as unitary subject matter for art; that the camera allows unmediated images into its frame; that photographs are neutral, "authentic" images of the world.

"I Am Not a Camera" dispels such notions of photographic objectivity and veracity:

> To call our sight Vision
> implies that, to us,
> all objects are subjects.

What we have not named
or beheld as a symbol
escapes our notice.

. . . .

Instructive as it may be to peer through lenses:
each time we do, though, we should apologise
to the remote or the small for intruding
upon their quiddities.

The camera records
visual facts: i.e.,
all may be fictions.

. . . .

On the screen we can only
witness human behavior:
Choice is for camera-crews.

The camera may
do justice to laughter, but must
degrade sorrow.[5]

These parables of perception raise several pertinent questions about documentary representation. For example, what perceptual biases are concealed when we call our observations of others documentary vision? Would coal miners have received such visual attention during Britain's depression had they not symbolized a hypermasculinity for documentary observers and viewers? For whom does the voyeuristic act of "peering through lenses" prove "instructive"? What might we learn if we directed these lenses away from "the remote or the small"? What interventions might camera crews make besides taking pictures? Ultimately for Auden, documentary photography reveals more about the culture that produces it than about those who appear within its restrictive frames.

As one of the thirties' defining voices, Auden proves indispensable for understanding socially engaged art in our century. His appropriations and interrogations of documentary discourse reveal the crisis of representation that accompanied the decade's socioeconomic crises. The 1930s continue to shape our culture's representation of social problems, a cross-century dialogue we can see in such documentary texts as Beatrix Campbell's *Wigan Pier Revisited: Poverty and Politics in the 80s* and Dale Maharidge and Michael Williamson's *And Their Children after Them* (a "sequel" to *Let Us Now Praise Famous Men*). Through his alternative models that offer verbal and visual critiques from *within* thirties documentary practice, Auden compels further returns to—and recoveries from—this troubling decade and its haunting images.

NOTES

1. Introduction

1. Jenkins, "Goodbye, 1939," 97. President Clinton quoted the final stanza of "In Memory of W. B. Yeats" in his address to the White House Correspondents Association dinner on 29 April 1995.

2. Auden, *Collected Poems*, 454, 646.

3. Kermode, *History and Value*, 47.

4. Cunard, quoted in Cunningham, *Spanish Front*, 51.

5. Auden, quoted in Cunningham, *Spanish Front*, 52.

6. Heaney, *Government of the Tongue*, 107; Auden, *Selected Poems*, 82.

7. Auden, *Selected Poems*, 82; Smith, *W. H. Auden*, 24.

8. News items appear under the journalists' names in the bibliography (Barry, Nyhan, Bell); Mendelson, Preface, xxiii.

9. Caesar, *Dividing Lines*, 3.

10. Brantlinger, *Crusoe's Footprints*, 16.

11. Swann, *British Documentary Film Movement*, 55, 63; Aitken, *Film and Reform*, 179.

12. Rotha, *Documentary Film*, 210.

13. Quoted in Calder and Sheridan, *Speak for Yourself*, 4; Auden and MacNeice, *Letters from Iceland*, 253.

14. Auden, *English Auden*, 22.

15. Auden, *English Auden*, 22; Branson and Heinemann, *Britain in the 1930s*, 102.

16. Priestley, *English Journey*, 261.

17. Auden, *English Auden*, 22; Grierson, *Grierson on Documentary*, 205; Priestley, *English Journey*, 80, emphasis added; Orwell, *Road to Wigan Pier*, 109, emphasis added.

18. Grierson, *Grierson on Documentary*, 142; Walkowitz, *City of Dreadful Delight*, 26; Smith, *W. H. Auden*, 74.

19. Mendelson, *Early Auden*, 34; Stott, *Documentary Expression and Thirties America*, 56.

20. Nichols, *Representing Reality*, xi.

21. Arthur, "Jargons of Authenticity," 127.

22. Rabinowitz, *They Must Be Represented,* 55; Winston, *Claiming the Real,* 251.

2. Documentary and Masculinity

1. Tate et al., "Sixteen Comments on Auden," 27; Barnouw, *Documentary,* 91; Miles and Smith, *Cinema, Literature and Society,* 189.

2. Cunningham, *British Writers of the Thirties,* 11; Trotter, *Making of the Reader,* 114.

3. Dodd, "Lowryscapes," 17; Stallybrass and White, *Politics and Poetics of Transgression,* 5.

4. Stevenson, "Myth and Reality," 92; Branson and Heinemann, *Britain in the 1930s,* 99.

5. There are some exceptions. For example, some of the E.M.B. and G.P.O. Film Unit's productions stress economic prosperity; *Industrial Britain* counters the coal mining sequence with an upbeat portrayal of the new steel industries, and *The Way to the Sea* celebrates the new electric railway from London to Southhampton.

6. Stallybrass and White, *Politics and Poetics of Transgression,* 5–6.

7. Stevenson, "Myth and Reality," 94; Colls and Dodd, "Representing the Nation," 25.

8. This quotation from the voice-over narration (and those that follow) comes from my viewing notes on *Industrial Britain,* now available on Kino Video's *E.M.B. Classics,* vol. 1 (1992).

9. Walkowitz, *City of Dreadful Delight,* 21; Rabinowitz, *They Must Be Represented,* 43.

10. Dodd, "Lowryscapes," 20; Orwell, *Road to Wigan Pier,* 168.

11. Orwell, *Road to Wigan Pier,* 24, 30, 22.

12. Barker et al., "Sixteen Comments on Auden," 24, 27.

13. Rotha, *Documentary Film,* 118, 193, emphasis added; Grierson, *Grierson on Documentary,* 217, 208, 181; Nichols, *Representing Reality,* 72.

14. Branson and Heinemann, *Britain in the 1930s,* 120; Auden, *English Auden,* 316.

15. Auden, *English Auden,* 376, 316, 236, 376; Ruskin, "Savageness of Gothic Architecture," 1284.

16. Priestley, *English Journey,* 175–76, emphasis added; Ruskin, "Savageness of Gothic Architecture," 1283, emphasis added.

17. Priestley, *English Journey,* 175, 179.

18. Auden, *English Auden,* 316; Morris, quoted in Thompson, *William Morris,* 101; *Industrial Britain,* viewing notes (see note 8 above), emphasis added; Priestley, *English Journey,* 169, 174, 184, emphasis added; Colls and Dodd, "Representing the Nation," 25.

19. Stansky, *William Morris,* 31.

20. Priestley, *English Journey,* 175.

21. With the exception of a few opening measures, the entire score of *Coriolan* is audible throughout the film's glassmaking sequence; an excerpt from

Beethoven's Fifth Symphony sounds during the closing moments of *Industrial Britain's* steelmaking sequence. For a brief discussion of Grierson's music selections for *Drifters*, see Aitken, *Film and Reform*, 108.

22. Grierson, *Grierson on Documentary*, 140.

23. Priestley, *English Journey*, 162, 163. Priestley's diverted paragraph ends, "This is, however, by the way"; the subsequent paragraph returns the narrator to the designated subject of the Potteries towns.

24. Kuhn, "British Documentary," 32; Grierson, *Grierson on Documentary*, 139; Rotha, *Documentary Film*, 129; Grierson, 201; Kuhn, 26; Swann, *British Documentary Film Movement*, 42.

25. Sidney, "Defense of Poesy," 607, 613; Auden, *English Auden*, 336; Yeats, *Selected Poems*, 192.

26. Madge, "Oxford Collective Poem," 16, emphasis added; Auden, *Dyer's Hand*, 77.

27. Auden, *English Auden*, 316.

28. Auden, *English Auden*, 316, emphasis added; Ruskin, "Savageness of Gothic Architecture," 1286.

29. Priestley, *English Journey*, 179, emphasis added; Orwell, *Road to Wigan Pier*, 32–33; Priestley, 183–84.

30. Sedgwick, *Between Men*, 1, 23.

31. Orwell, *Road to Wigan Pier*, 23; Woods, *Articulate Flesh*, 30, 31.

32. Auden, "I chose this lean country," *English Auden*, 440; Mendelson, *Early Auden*, 225–26; Auden, "The chimneys are smoking," *English Auden*, 117–18.

33. Barnouw, *Documentary*, 90; see Rotha, *Documentary Diary*.

34. Koven, "From Rough Lads to Hooligans," 373.

35. Their work with Holmes was the 1937 film *The Way to the Sea;* for more information on the Britten-Auden collaboration, see Mitchell, *Britten and Auden in the Thirties.*

36. Cunningham, *British Writers of the Thirties*, 150, emphasis added.

37. Weeks, *Sex, Politics and Society*, 112; Woods, *Articulate Flesh*, 1; Ellenzweig, *Homoerotic Photograph*, 2.

38. Colls and Dodd, "Representing the Nation," 24.

39. Miles and Smith, *Cinema, Literature and Society*, 191; Potter, quoted in Colls and Dodd, "Representing the Nation," 25.

40. Nichols, *Ideology and the Image*, 196, 197. Quotations from the voice-over narration of *Coal Face* come from my viewing notes. The film is available on videocassette from the General Post Office's Film and Video Department.

41. Mendelson quotes the full men's chorus in the "Textual Notes" section of Auden, *Plays, and Other Dramatic Writings*, 665; Sedgwick, *Between Men*, 21.

42. Auden, *Plays, and Other Dramatic Writings*, 421; Lawrence, *Complete Short Stories*, 1:268, emphasis added.

43. McDiarmid, "Liberating the Pseudoese," 143; Auden, *Collected Poems*, 470; Sinfield, *Cultural Politics—Queer Reading*, 60; Butler, *Gender Trouble*, 25.

44. Auden, *Plays, and Other Dramatic Writings*, 261–62.

45. Koven, "From Rough Lads to Hooligans," 373; Carpenter, *W. H. Auden,* 90, 96; Sedgwick, *Epistemology of the Closet,* 1.

46. Isherwood, *Lions and Shadows,* 75–76; Priestley, *English Journey,* 261.

47. One of the last G.P.O. Film Unit productions, *The First Days* (Cavalcanti, 1939), depicted the East and West Ends of London during the outbreak of World War II. Under the Ministry of Information, the filmmaking group became the Crown Film Unit, where Mass-Observer–G.P.O. filmmaker Humphrey Jennings codirected *Listen to Britain* (1941) and directed *Fires Were Started* (1943).

48. Orwell, *Road to Wigan Pier,* 110.

49. Quotations from the voice-over narration of *Night Mail* come from my viewing notes. Incidentally, Miles and Smith are mistaken in asserting that this segment of *Night Mail's* narration accompanies "the same long shot of the racing train, with no visual reference to these passing towns at all"; see *Cinema, Literature and Society,* 191.

50. Auden, *Plays, and Other Dramatic Writings,* 667.

51. Auden, *Plays, and Other Dramatic Writings,* 422, 423.

52. Auden, *Plays, and Other Dramatic Writings,* 423; Miles and Smith, *Cinema, Literature and Society,* 191.

53. Smith, *W. H. Auden,* 1, 2.

54. Buell, *W. H. Auden as a Social Poet,* 137, emphasis added; McDiarmid, *Auden's Apologies for Poetry,* x.

55. Auden, *Dyer's Hand,* 73, 89, 88.

56. Hynes, *Auden Generation,* 135; Auden, *English Auden,* 137.

57. Woods, *Articulate Flesh,* 169, 174; Auden, *English Auden,* 354.

58. Aitken, *Film and Reform,* 5; Willemen, "Presentation," 5, 2.

59. Kuhn, "British Documentary," 27.

60. Kuhn, "British Documentary," 30; Miles and Smith, *Cinema, Literature and Society,* 191, 190; Willemen, "Presentation," 2.

61. Cunningham et al., "'Communist to Others,'" 185; Auden, "Communist to Others," 173.

3. Documentary and Modernism

1. Auden and MacNeice, *Letters from Iceland,* 226. All references follow Faber and Faber's 1937 edition; Paragon House's 1990 reprint varies from the original in page numbering and photo placement.

2. Tolley, *Poetry of the Thirties,* 305; Fussell, *Abroad,* 219; Buell, *W. H. Auden as a Social Poet,* 139; Paulin, "*Letters from Iceland,*" 66.

3. Muir, Review, 154.

4. Auden and MacNeice, *Letters from Iceland,* 21; Hunter, *Image and Word,* 157.

5. Cunningham, *British Writers of the Thirties,* 83; Sackville-West, "On Being Mainly Amused," 242; "Cooling Waters," 244; Williamson, *Consuming Passions,* 122. Incidentally, the second English and American editions of *Letters from Iceland* appeared without photographs; the map of Iceland is the book's only illustration.

6. Mendelson provided this information in a letter to me (1 August 1987).

7. Wright, *W. H. Auden,* 76.

8. Auden and MacNeice, *Letters from Iceland,* 17; Hynes, *Auden Generation,* 212–13.

9. Grierson, *Grierson on Documentary,* 206.

10. Auden and MacNeice, *Letters from Iceland,* 149–50, 223.

11. Auden and MacNeice, *Letters from Iceland,* 216, 195, 194.

12. Sontag, *On Photography,* 55.

13. Auden, *English Auden,* 355; Rotha, *Documentary Film,* 130.

14. Tagg, *Burden of Representation,* 6; Rotha, *Documentary Film,* 7; Grierson, *Grierson on Documentary,* 201, 205.

15. Nichols, *Ideology and the Image,* 238; Auden, *English Auden,* 354.

16. Auden, *English Auden,* 355.

17. Auden and MacNeice, *Letters from Iceland,* 67.

18. Auden and MacNeice, *Letters from Iceland,* 21; Clifford, *Predicament of Culture,* 146.

19. Auden and MacNeice, *Letters from Iceland,* 22; Rotha, *Documentary Film,* 62.

20. Auden and MacNeice, *Letters from Iceland,* 18, 226, 25.

21. Auden and MacNeice, *Letters from Iceland,* 71–72, 62, 74, 73.

22. Auden and MacNeice, *Letters from Iceland,* 137.

23. Auden and MacNeice, *Letters from Iceland,* 173; Yates, "Iceland 1936," 63; Auden and MacNeice, *Letters from Iceland,* 25–26; Fuller, *Reader's Guide,* 113–14.

24. Jameson, quoted in Hynes, *Auden Generation,* 271.

25. Greenberg, *Quest for the Necessary,* 80; Mendelson, *Early Auden,* 311.

26. Auden and MacNeice, *Letters from Iceland,* 147.

27. Auden and MacNeice, *Letters from Iceland,* 91.

28. Auden and MacNeice, *Letters from Iceland,* 91.

29. Auden and MacNeice, *Letters from Iceland,* 91; Barthes, *Empire of Signs,* xi.

30. Auden and MacNeice, *Letters from Iceland,* 92.

31. Auden and MacNeice, *Letters from Iceland,* 93; Mendelson, *Early Auden,* 314.

32. Beach, *Making of the Auden Canon,* 140; Auden and MacNeice, *Letters from Iceland,* 222.

33. Auden and MacNeice, *Letters from Iceland,* 220, 221, 220; Fussell, *Abroad,* 219.

34. Auden and MacNeice, *Letters from Iceland,* 222, 142.

35. Auden and MacNeice, *Letters from Iceland,* 223, 221, 223; Rotha, *Documentary Film,* 77.

36. Auden and MacNeice, *Letters from Iceland,* 224.

37. Cunningham, *British Writers of the Thirties,* 329; Grierson, *Grierson on Documentary,* 205.

38. Auden and MacNeice, *Letters from Iceland,* 224.

39. Auden and MacNeice, *Letters from Iceland,* 224; Tagg, *Burden of Representation,* 8.

40. Fussell, *Abroad,* 220; Orwell, *Inside the Whale,* 27.

4. Documentary and Cultural Memory

1. Osborne, *W. H. Auden*, 133.

2. Orwell, *Inside the Whale*, 36.

3. Cockburn, "Conversation," 51.

4. Dodds, *Missing Persons*, 133.

5. Auden, *Selected Poems*, 53, 54, 55.

6. Orwell, *Inside the Whale*, 37; Kermode, *History and Value*, 78; Smith, "Missing Dates," 155; Hynes, *Auden Generation*, 252; Mander, *The Writer and Commitment*, 69; Ford, *Poet's War*, 20.

7. Spender, *Poems for Spain*, 8, 11, 13; Cunningham, *Spanish Civil War Verse*, 73; Cunningham, *Spanish Front*, xxxi.

8. Mendelson, *Early Auden*, 319, 322; Thompson, "Outside the Whale," 148.

9. Trotter, *Making of the Reader*, 116, 113; Auden, *Selected Poems*, 54; Smith, "Missing Dates," 161, 165.

10. Hemingway, "Dispatches," 25; Ivens, *Camera and I*, 115; Jenkins, "Auden and Spain," 91.

11. Waugh, "Joris Ivens' *The Spanish Earth*," 121; Day-Lewis, Review, 236; Mendelson, *Early Auden*, 349; Winsten and Masters, quoted in Ivens, *Camera and I*, 133, 134.

12. Powers, *Three Farmers*, 81.

13. Auden, *Selected Poems*, 51, 52.

14. Auden, *Selected Poems*, 53, 54; Auden, *Plays, and Other Dramatic Writings*, 582.

15. Waugh, "Water, Blood, and War," 18.

16. Alexander, *Film on the Left*, 155.

17. Waugh, "Joris Ivens' *The Spanish Earth*," 130; Auden, *Selected Poems*, 53.

18. This quotation from *The Spanish Earth*'s commentary, and those that follow, come from my viewing notes.

19. Warner, "Arms in Spain," 50; Howard, "For Those with Investments in Spain," 77–78; the quotation from *Heart of Spain* comes from my viewing notes.

20. Auden, *English Auden*, 361; Hemingway, "Dispatches," 27, 67; Waugh, "Joris Ivens' *The Spanish Earth*," 130.

21. Ivens, *Camera and I*, 128; Auden, *English Auden*, 329.

22. Auden, *Selected Poems*, 52, 52–53; Smith, "Missing Dates," 170.

23. Auden, *Selected Poems*, 53.

24. Auden, *Selected Poems*, 53–54, emphasis added, 55.

25. *Spanish Earth*, viewing notes; Waugh, "Joris Ivens' *The Spanish Earth*," 123.

26. Alexander, *Film on the Left*, 155.

27. Auden, *Selected Poems*, 54.

28. Barthes, *Camera Lucida*, 96, 95.

29. Meyers and Leyda, "Joris Ivens," 166.

30. Warner, "The Tourist Looks at Spain," 68; Hynes, *Auden Generation*, 133.

31. Woolf, *Three Guineas*, 10–11.

32. Auden, *Selected Poems*, 55; Waugh, "Joris Ivens' *The Spanish Earth*," 129.

33. Auden, *Selected Poems,* 54; Spender, *Poems for Spain,* 7; Ivens, *Camera and I,* 118; Capa, *Slightly out of Focus,* 170.

34. Hayes, "Spanish Civil War in *Life* Magazine," 62; Powers, *Three Farmers,* 257.

35. Auden, *Selected Poems,* 55; Whelan, *Robert Capa,* 99–100; Knightley, *First Casualty,* 209, 219.

36. Whelan, *Robert Capa,* 95.

37. Whelan, *Robert Capa,* 100.

38. Grosvenor and Kemp, "Spain's Falling Soldier Really Did Die," 3.

39. Lacouture, Introduction; Thomas, *Spanish Civil War,* 303; Auden, *Selected Poems,* 53–54. Although Thomas quotes the poem accurately for the most part, he does misrepresent Auden's activities in Spain and misattributes other quotations to him. Mendelson points to these inaccuracies in *Early Auden.*

40. Berger, *About Looking,* 60, 63, 62, 57; Smith, "Missing Dates," 171, 172.

41. Heinemann, "English Poetry and the War in Spain," 64.

5. Documentary Dilemmas

1. Isherwood, *Christopher and His Kind,* 289.

2. Swingler, "On Being Uninvolved," 291; Hynes, *Auden Generation,* 342.

3. Waugh, "On a Pantomime Appearance," 289; Kirstein, "On the Greatest Poetry of Our Speech," 297; Wright, *W. H. Auden,* 86.

4. Auden and Isherwood, *Journey to a War,* 112. I cite the recent Paragon House edition of the book, which follows the original edition's pagination.

5. Auden and Isherwood, *Journey to a War,* 92, 175.

6. Auden and Isherwood, *Journey to a War,* 275; O'Neill and Reeves, *Auden, MacNeice, Spender,* 178.

7. Hynes, *Auden Generation,* 343.

8. Auden and Isherwood, *Journey to a War,* 206; Waugh, "On a Pantomime Appearance," 289; Hynes, *Auden Generation,* 342.

9. Auden and Isherwood, "Chinese Diary," 95; Auden and Isherwood, "Meeting the Japanese," 10; Plomer, Review, 292.

10. Auden and Isherwood, *Journey to a War,* 112; Auden and Isherwood, "Chinese Diary," 95.

11. Auden and Isherwood, *Journey to a War,* 114–15.

12. Auden and Isherwood, *Journey to a War,* 115; Shloss, *In Visible Light,* 20.

13. Auden and Isherwood, *Journey to a War,* 222; Swingler, "On Being Uninvolved," 291.

14. Auden and Isherwood, *Journey to a War,* 281, 284.

15. Auden and Isherwood, *Journey to a War,* 285, 253, 202.

16. Fussell, *Abroad,* 222; Swingler, "On Being Uninvolved," 291.

17. Butler, "Imitation and Gender Insubordination," 20–21.

18. Isherwood, *Christopher and His Kind,* 264.

19. Koestenbaum, *Double Talk,* 3.

20. Auden, *English Auden,* 233; Auden and Isherwood, *Journey to a War,* 53; Auden, *English Auden,* 233.

21. Auden and Isherwood, *Journey to a War,* 53, 77, 79; Newton, "Role Models," 48–49.

22. Isherwood, *Christopher and His Kind,* 308; Auden and Isherwood, *Journey to a War,* 237, 123.

23. Plomer, Review, 293; Auden and Isherwood, *Journey to a War,* 178, 179, 183.

24. Babuscio, "Camp and the Gay Sensibility," 25.

25. Auden and Isherwood, *Journey to a War,* 62; Said, *Orientalism,* 158; Auden and Isherwood, *Journey to a War,* 104; Isherwood, *Christopher and His Kind,* 301.

26. Phelan, *Unmarked,* 35.

27. Auden and Isherwood, *Journey to a War,* 73; Babuscio, "Camp and the Gay Sensibility," 24.

28. Auden and Isherwood, *Journey to a War,* 156, 207.

29. Butler, "Imitation and Gender Insubordination," 23; Edelman, *Homographesis,* 14, 10.

30. Auden and Isherwood, *Journey to a War,* 116.

31. Auden and Isherwood, *Journey to a War,* 292, 295, 296, 297; Smith, *W. H. Auden,* 110; Greenberg, *Quest for the Necessary,* 88; Auden and Isherwood, *Journey to a War,* 271.

32. Auden and Isherwood, *Journey to a War,* 298, 282; Smith, *W. H. Auden,* 115.

33. Boone, "Vacation Cruises," 90; Auden and Isherwood, *Journey to a War,* 20.

34. Auden and Isherwood, *Journey to a War,* 291; Said, *Orientalism,* 11; Kirstein, "On the Greatest Poetry of Our Speech," 297; Swingler, "On Being Uninvolved," 291.

35. Auden and Isherwood, *Journey to a War,* 30; Hynes, *Auden Generation,* 342.

36. Auden and Isherwood, "Meeting the Japanese," 10.

37. Said, *Orientalism,* 43; Auden and Isherwood, "Escales," 126.

38. Lowe, *Critical Terrains,* 28, 2.

39. Auden and Isherwood, *Journey to a War,* 39, emphasis added; "Review of *The Chinese Bungalow,*" 10, emphasis added; Lowe, *Critical Terrains,* 2.

40. Auden and Isherwood, *Journey to a War,* 234; Pratt, *Imperial Eyes,* 201, 204–5.

41. Auden and Isherwood, *Journey to a War,* 23; Smith, *W. H. Auden,* 110.

42. Auden and Isherwood, *Journey to a War,* 243, 245; Sontag, "Project for a Trip to China," 150.

43. Auden and Isherwood, *Journey to a War,* 252.

44. Auden and Isherwood, *Journey to a War,* 291.

45. In the Picture Commentary, each of these photographs is paired with another that shares the same caption.

46. Said, *Orientalism,* 44.

47. Auden, *English Auden,* 329; Rowan, "Asia out of Focus," 36; Grierson, *Grierson on Documentary,* 210.

48. McDiarmid, "Liberating the Pseudoese," 138, 139.

49. Auden and Isherwood, *Journey to a War,* 299–300; Auden, *Plays, and Other Dramatic Writings,* 668.

50. Wright, quoted in Sussex, *Rise and Fall,* 71–72.

51. *Industrial Britain,* viewing notes; Cunningham, *British Writers of the Thirties,* 328.

52. Grierson, *Grierson on Documentary,* 210, 203, emphasis added, 215.

6. Afterword

1. Auden, *Selected Poems,* 86.

2. Stern published his own observations in *The Hidden Damage* (1947), referring to Auden as "Mervyn." Auden, "Squares and Oblongs," 174.

3. Auden, *Selected Poems,* 191.

4. Auden et al., "Authors Take Sides on Vietnam," 11.

5. Isherwood, *Goodbye to Berlin,* 13; Auden, *Collected Poems,* 630–31.

FILMOGRAPHY

Coal Face. Dir. Alberto Cavalcanti. Great Britain, G.P.O. Film Unit, 1935.

The Face of Britain. Dir. Paul Rotha. Great Britain, G-B Instructional, 1935.

The Good Fight: The Abraham Lincoln Brigade in the Spanish Civil War. Dir. Noel Buckner, Mary Dore, and Sam Sills. U.S.A., 1987.

Heart of Spain. Scenarized and ed. Paul Strand and Leo Hurwitz. U.S.A., Frontier Films, 1937.

Industrial Britain. Dir. Robert Flaherty and John Grierson. Great Britain, E.M.B. Film Unit, 1933.

The Mine. Dir. J. B. Holmes. Great Britain, G-B Instructional, 1935.

Night Mail. Dir. Basil Wright and Harry Watt. Great Britain, G.P.O. Film Unit, 1936.

Song of Ceylon. Dir. Basil Wright. Great Britain, E.M.B. Film Unit, 1934.

The Spanish Earth. Dir. Joris Ivens. U.S.A., Contemporary Historians, 1937.

BIBLIOGRAPHY

Aitken, Ian. *Film and Reform: John Grierson and the Documentary Film Movement.* London: Routledge, 1990.

Alexander, William. *Film on the Left: American Documentary Film from 1931 to 1942.* Princeton: Princeton Univ. Press, 1981.

Arthur, Paul. "Jargons of Authenticity (Three American Moments)." In *Theorizing Documentary,* ed. Michael Renov, 108–34. New York: Routledge, 1993.

Auden, W. H. *Collected Poems.* Ed. Edward Mendelson. New York: Random House, 1976.

————. "A Communist to Others." In *New Country: Prose and Poetry by the Authors of "New Signatures."* Ed. Michael Roberts. London: Hogarth, 1933.

————. *The Dyer's Hand and Other Essays.* New York: Vintage, 1968.

————. *The English Auden: Poems, Essays and Dramatic Writings 1927–1939.* Ed. Edward Mendelson. New York: Random House, 1977.

————. *Juvenilia: Poems 1922–1928.* Ed. Katherine Bucknell. Princeton: Princeton Univ. Press, 1994.

————. *Plays, and Other Dramatic Writings by W. H. Auden, 1928–1938.* Vol. 1 of *The Complete Works of W. H. Auden.* Ed. Edward Mendelson. Princeton: Princeton Univ. Press, 1988.

————. *Selected Poems.* New ed. Ed. Edward Mendelson. New York: Vintage, 1979.

————. "Squares and Oblongs." In *Poets at Work,* ed. Charles D. Abbott, 163–81. New York: Harcourt, 1948.

Auden, W. H., and Christopher Isherwood. "Chinese Diary." *New Republic,* 1 June 1938, 94–97.

————. *The Dog beneath the Skin. Plays, and Other Dramatic Writings by W. H. Auden, 1928–1938.* Vol. 1 of *The Complete Works of W. H. Auden.* Ed. Edward Mendelson. Princeton: Princeton Univ. Press, 1988.

————. "Escales." *Harpers Bazaar,* October 1938, 78–79, 126–27.

————. *Journey to a War.* 1939. Reprint, New York: Paragon House, 1990.

————. "Meeting the Japanese." *New Masses,* 16 August 1938, 10.

Auden, W. H., and Louis MacNeice. *Letters from Iceland.* London: Faber and Faber, 1937.

Auden, W. H., et al. "Authors Take Sides on Vietnam." *Envoy* 1 (1967): 10–13.

Babuscio, Jack. "Camp and the Gay Sensibility." In *Camp Grounds: Style and Homosexuality,* ed. David Bergman, 19–38. Amherst: Univ. of Massachusetts Press. 1993.

Barker, George, et al. "Sixteen Comments on Auden." *New Verse* 26–27 (1937): 23–30.

Barnouw, Erik. *Documentary: A History of the Non-fiction Film.* London: Oxford Univ. Press, 1974.

Barry, John. "Now for a Real VE Day." *Newsweek,* 22 May 1995, 28.

Barthes, Roland. *Camera Lucida: Reflections on Photography.* Trans. Richard Howard. New York: Hill & Wang, 1981.

———. *Empire of Signs.* Trans. Richard Howard. New York: Hill & Wang, 1982.

Beach, Joseph Warren. *The Making of the Auden Canon.* Minneapolis: Univ. of Minnesota Press, 1957.

Bell, Ian. "Alas, but We Cannot Help or Pardon." *Herald* (Glasgow), 1 June 1995.

Berger, John. *About Looking.* New York: Pantheon, 1980.

Boly, John R. *Reading Auden: The Returns of Caliban.* Ithaca: Cornell Univ. Press, 1991.

Boone, Joseph A. "Vacation Cruises; or, The Homoerotics of Orientalism." *PMLA* 110 (1995): 89–107.

Branson, Noreen, and Margot Heinemann. *Britain in the 1930s.* New York: Praeger, 1971.

Brantlinger, Patrick. *Crusoe's Footprints: Cultural Studies in Britain and America.* New York: Routledge, 1990.

Bucknell, Katherine, and Nicholas Jenkins, eds. *W. H. Auden, "The Map of All My Youth": Early Works, Friends, and Influences.* Auden Studies 1. Oxford: Oxford Univ. Press, 1990.

Buell, Frederick. *W. H. Auden as a Social Poet.* Ithaca: Cornell Univ. Press, 1973.

Butler, Judith. *Gender Trouble: Feminism and the Subversion of Identity.* New York: Routledge, 1990.

———. "Imitation and Gender Insubordination." In *Inside/Out: Lesbian Theories, Gay Theories,* ed. Diana Fuss, 13–31. New York: Routledge, 1991.

Caesar, Adrian. *Dividing Lines: Poetry, Class and Ideology in the 1930s.* Manchester: Manchester Univ. Press, 1991.

Calder, Angus, and Dorothy Sheridan, eds. *Speak for Yourself: A Mass-Observation Anthology, 1937–49.* London: Jonathan Cape, 1984.

Capa, Robert. *Slightly out of Focus.* New York: Henry Holt, 1947.

Carpenter, Humphrey. *W. H. Auden: A Biography.* Boston: Houghton Mifflin, 1981.

Clifford, James. *The Predicament of Culture: Twentieth-Century Ethnography, Literature, and Art.* Cambridge: Harvard Univ. Press, 1988.

Cockburn, Claud. "A Conversation with Claud Cockburn." *Review* 11–12 (1964): 51–53.

Colls, Robert, and Philip Dodd. "Representing the Nation: British Documentary Film, 1930–45." *Screen* 26 (1985): 21–33.

"Cooling Waters." Review of *Letters from Iceland,* by W. H. Auden and Louis MacNeice. In *W. H. Auden: The Critical Heritage,* ed. John Haffenden, 242–45. London: Routledge & Kegan Paul, 1983.

Cunningham, Valentine. *British Writers of the Thirties.* Oxford: Oxford Univ. Press, 1989.

———. Introduction to *The Penguin Book of Spanish Civil War Verse.* Harmondsworth: Penguin, 1980.

———. Introduction to *Spanish Front: Writers on the Civil War.* Oxford: Oxford Univ. Press, 1986.

Cunningham, Valentine, et al. "'A Communist to Others': A Symposium." In *W. H. Auden, "The Map of All My Youth": Early Works, Friends, and Influences,* ed. Katherine Bucknell and Nicholas Jenkins, 173–95. Auden Studies 1. Oxford: Oxford Univ. Press, 1990.

Day-Lewis, Cecil. Review of *Spain,* by W. H. Auden. In *W. H. Auden: The Critical Heritage,* ed. John Haffenden, 236. London: Routledge & Kegan Paul, 1983.

Dodd, Philip. "Lowryscapes: Recent Writings about the 'North.'" *Critical Quarterly* 32, no. 2 (1990): 17–28.

Dodds, E. R. *Missing Persons.* Oxford: Clarendon, 1977.

Edelman, Lee. *Homographesis: Essays in Gay Literary and Cultural Theory.* New York: Routledge, 1994.

Eliot, T. S. *The Complete Poems and Plays, 1909–1950.* New York: Harcourt Brace, 1971.

Ellenzweig, Allen. *The Homoerotic Photograph.* New York: Columbia Univ. Press, 1992.

Ford, Hugh D. *A Poet's War: British Poets and the Spanish Civil War.* Philadelphia: Univ. of Pennsylvania Press, 1965.

Fuller, John. *A Reader's Guide to W. H. Auden.* New York: Farrar, Straus & Giroux, 1970.

Fussell, Paul. *Abroad: British Literary Traveling between the Wars.* Oxford: Oxford Univ. Press, 1980.

Greenberg, Herbert. *Quest for the Necessary: W. H. Auden and the Dilemma of Divided Consciousness.* Cambridge: Harvard Univ. Press, 1968.

Grierson, John. *Grierson on Documentary.* Ed. Forsyth Hardy. Rev. ed. Berkeley: Univ. of California Press, 1966.

Grosvenor, Rita, and Arnold Kemp. "Spain's Falling Soldier Really Did Die That Day," *Observer,* 1 September 1996.

Hayes, Aden. "The Spanish Civil War in *Life* Magazine." In *The Spanish Civil War and the Visual Arts,* ed. Kathleen Vernon, 62–70. Western Societies Program Occasional Paper 24. Ithaca: Center for International Studies, Cornell University: 1990.

Heaney, Seamus. *The Government of the Tongue: Selected Prose, 1978–87.* New York: Farrar, Straus & Giroux, 1989.

Heinemann, Margot. "English Poetry and the War in Spain: Some Records of a Generation." In *"¡No Pasarán!" Art, Literature and the Spanish Civil War,* ed. Stephen M. Hart, 46–64. London: Tamesis, 1988.

Hemingway, Ernest. "Hemingway's Spanish Civil War Dispatches." Ed. William Braasch Watson. *Hemingway Review* 7, no. 2 (1988): 23–26, 26–29, 63–68.

Howard, Brian. "For Those with Investments in Spain: 1937." In *Poems for Spain,* ed. Stephen Spender and John Lehmann, 77–78. London: Hogarth, 1939.

Hunter, Jefferson. *Image and Word: The Interaction of Twentieth-Century Photographs and Texts.* Cambridge: Harvard Univ. Press, 1987.

Hynes, Samuel. *The Auden Generation: Literature and Politics in England in the 1930s.* Princeton: Princeton Univ. Press, 1976.

Isherwood, Christopher. *Christopher and His Kind, 1929–1939.* New York: Farrar, Straus & Giroux, 1977.

———. *Goodbye to Berlin.* London: Hogarth, 1939.

———. *Lions and Shadows.* 1938. Reprint, New York: Pegasus, 1969.

Ivens, Joris. *The Camera and I.* New York: International, 1969.

Jenkins, Nicholas. "Auden and Spain." In *W. H. Auden: "The Map of All My Youth," Early Works, Friends and Influences,* ed. Katherine Bucknell and Nicholas Jenkins, 88–93. Auden Studies 1. Oxford: Clarendon, 1990.

———. "Goodbye, 1939." *New Yorker,* 1 April 1996, 88–97.

Kermode, Frank. *History and Value.* New York: Oxford Univ. Press, 1988.

Kirstein, Lincoln. "On the Greatest Poetry of Our Speech, Poets under Fire." Review of *Journey to a War,* by W. H. Auden and Christopher Isherwood. In *W. H. Auden: The Critical Heritage,* ed. John Haffenden, 297–300. London: Routledge & Kegan Paul, 1983.

Knightley, Phillip. *The First Casualty, from the Crimea to Vietnam: The War Correspondent as Hero, Propagandist, and Myth Maker.* New York: Harcourt Brace, 1975.

Koestenbaum, Wayne. *Double Talk: The Erotics of Male Literary Collaboration.* New York: Routledge, 1989.

Koven, Seth. "From Rough Lads to Hooligans: Boy Life, National Culture and Social Reform." In *Nationalisms and Sexualities,* ed. Andrew Parker et al., 365–92. New York: Routledge, 1992.

Kuhn, Annette. "British Documentary in the 1930s and 'Independence': Recontextualising a Film Movement." In *British Cinema: Traditions of Independence,* ed. Don Macpherson and Paul Willemen, 24–32. London: British Film Institute, 1980.

Lacouture, Jean. Introduction to *Robert Capa.* Trans. Abigail Pollak. New York: Pantheon, 1989.

Lawrence, D. H. *The Complete Short Stories.* Vol. 1. Harmondsworth: Penguin, 1976.

———. *Poems.* Selected by Keith Sagar. Rev. ed. London: Penguin, 1986.

———. *Women in Love.* New York: Cambridge Univ. Press, 1987.

Lowe, Lisa. *Critical Terrains: French and British Orientalisms.* Ithaca: Cornell Univ. Press, 1991.

MacLeish, Archibald. *Land of the Free.* 1938. Reprint, with introduction by A. D. Coleman, New York: Da Capo, 1977.

Madge, Charles. "The Oxford Collective Poem." *New Verse* 25 (1937): 16–19.

Madge, Charles, et al. "Sixteen Comments on Auden." *New Verse* 26–27 (1937): 23–30.

Mander, John. *The Writer and Commitment.* London: Secker & Warburg, 1961.

McDiarmid, Lucy. *Auden's Apologies for Poetry.* Princeton: Princeton Univ. Press, 1990.

———. "Liberating the Pseudoese." *Yale Review* 79 (1989): 136–46.

Mendelson, Edward. *Early Auden.* Cambridge: Harvard Univ. Press, 1983.

———. Preface to *Selected Poems,* by W. H. Auden. New ed. New York: Vintage, 1979.

Meyers, Sidney, and Jay Leyda. "Joris Ivens: Artist in Documentary." In *The Documentary Tradition: From Nanook to Woodstock,* ed. Lewis Jacobs, 158–66. New York: Hopkinson and Blake, 1971.

Miles, Peter, and Malcolm Smith. *Cinema, Literature and Society: Elite and Mass Culture in Interwar Britain.* London: Croom Helm, 1987.

Mitchell, Donald. *Britten and Auden in the Thirties: The Year 1936.* Seattle: Univ. of Washington Press, 1981.

Muir, Edwin. Review of *Letters from Iceland,* by W. H. Auden and Louis MacNeice. In *W. H. Auden: The Critical Heritage,* ed. John Haffenden, 247. London: Routledge & Kegan Paul, 1983.

Mulvey, Laura. "Visual Pleasure in Narrative Cinema." *Screen* 16, no. 3 (1975): 6–18.

Newton, Esther. "Role Models." In *Camp Grounds: Style and Homosexuality,* ed. David Bergman, 39–53. Amherst: Univ. of Massachusetts Press, 1993.

Nichols, Bill. *Ideology and the Image: Social Representation in the Cinema and Other Media.* Bloomington: Indiana Univ. Press, 1981.

———. *Representing Reality: Issues and Concepts in Documentary.* Bloomington: Indiana Univ. Press, 1991.

Nyhan, David. "Yugoslavia's Dark Cold Day." *Boston Globe,* 28 November 1991.

O'Neill, Michael, and Gareth Reeves. *Auden, MacNeice, Spender: The Thirties Poetry.* London: Macmillan, 1992.

Orwell, George. *Inside the Whale.* Harmondsworth: Penguin, 1957.

———. *The Road to Wigan Pier.* 1937. Reprint, New York: Harcourt Brace Jovanovich, 1958.

Osborne, Charles. *W. H. Auden: A Biography.* Boston: Houghton Mifflin, 1981.

Owen, Wilfred. *The Collected Poems of Wilfred Owen.* Ed. C. Day Lewis. New York: New Directions, 1965.

Paulin, Tom. "*Letters from Iceland:* Going North." *Renaissance and Modern Studies* 20 (1976): 65–80.

Phelan, Peggy. *Unmarked: The Politics of Performance.* London: Routledge, 1993.

Plomer, William. Review of *Journey to a War,* by W. H. Auden and Christopher Isherwood. In *W. H. Auden: The Critical Heritage,* ed. John Haffenden, 292–94. London: Routledge & Kegan Paul, 1983.

Powers, Richard. *Three Farmers on Their Way to a Dance.* New York: Beech Tree, 1985.

Pratt, Mary Louise. *Imperial Eyes: Travel Writing and Transculturation.* London: Routledge, 1992.

Priestley, J. B. *English Journey.* New York: Harper, 1934.

Rabinowitz, Paula. *They Must Be Represented: The Politics of Documentary.* London: Verso, 1994.

Review of *The Chinese Bungalow. Times* (London), 10 January 1929, 10.

Review of *Letters from Iceland,* by W. H. Auden and Louis MacNeice. In *W. H. Auden: The Critical Heritage,* ed. John Haffenden, 242–45. London: Routledge & Kegan Paul, 1983.

Rotha, Paul. *Documentary Diary: An Informal History of the British Documentary Film, 1928–1939.* New York: Hill & Wang, 1973.

———. *Documentary Film.* London: Faber and Faber, 1936.

Rowan, Mary M. "Asia out of Focus: Decoding Malraux's Orient." In *Witnessing André Malraux: Visions and Re-visions,* ed. Brian Thompson and Carl A. Viggiani, 30–39. Middletown CT: Wesleyan Univ. Press, 1984.

Ruskin, John. "The Savageness of Gothic Architecture" (from *The Stones of Venice*). In *The Norton Anthology of English Literature,* 6th ed., ed. M. H. Abrams, 2:1280–90. New York: W. W. Norton, 1993.

Sackville-West, Edward. "On Being Mainly Amused." Review of *Letters from Iceland,* by W. H. Auden and Louis MacNeice. In *W. H. Auden: The Critical Heritage,* ed. John Haffenden, 240–42. London: Routledge & Kegan Paul, 1983.

Said, Edward W. *Orientalism.* New York: Vintage, 1979.

Sedgwick, Eve Kosofsky. *Between Men: English Literature and Male Homosocial Desire.* New York: Columbia Univ. Press, 1985.

———. *Epistemology of the Closet.* Berkeley: Univ. of California Press, 1990.

Shloss, Carol. *In Visible Light: Photography and the American Writer, 1840–1940.* New York: Oxford Univ. Press, 1987.

Sidney, Philip. "The Defense of Poesy." In *The Renaissance in England: Nondramatic Prose and Verse of the Sixteenth Century,* ed. Hyder E. Rollins and Herschel Baker, 605–24. Lexington MA: Heath, 1954.

Sinfield, Alan. *Cultural Politics—Queer Reading.* Philadelphia: Univ. of Pennsylvania Press, 1994.

Smith, Stan. "Missing Dates: From *Spain 1937* to 'September 1, 1939.'" *Literature and History* 13 (1987): 155–74.

———. *W. H. Auden.* New York: Basil Blackwell, 1985.

Sontag, Susan. *On Photography.* New York: Farrar, Straus & Giroux, 1977.

———. "Project for a Trip to China." In *New Directions in Prose and Poetry 35,* ed. J. Laughlin, 130–51. New York: New Directions, 1977.

Spencer, Bernard, et al. "Sixteen Comments on Auden." *New Verse* 26–27 (1937): 23–30.

Spender, Stephen. Introduction to *Poems for Spain.* Ed. Stephen Spender and John Lehmann. London: Hogarth, 1939.

Stallybrass, Peter, and Allon White. *The Politics and Poetics of Transgression.* Ithaca: Cornell Univ. Press, 1986.

Stansky, Peter. *William Morris*. Oxford: Oxford Univ. Press, 1983.

Stevenson, John. "Myth and Reality: Britain in the 1930s." In *Crisis and Controversy: Essays in Honour of A. J. P. Taylor,* ed. Alan Sked and Chris Cook, 90–109. New York: St. Martin's, 1976.

Stott, William. *Documentary Expression and Thirties America*. London: Oxford Univ. Press, 1973.

Summerfield, Penny. "Mass-Observation: Social Research or Social Movement?" *Journal of Contemporary History* 20 (1985): 439–52.

Sussex, Elizabeth. *The Rise and Fall of British Documentary*. Berkeley: Univ. of California Press, 1975.

Swann, Paul. *The British Documentary Film Movement, 1926–1946*. Cambridge: Cambridge Univ. Press, 1989.

Swingler, Randall. "On Being Uninvolved: Two Intellectuals in China." Review of *Journey to a War,* by W. H. Auden and Christopher Isherwood. In *W. H. Auden: The Critical Heritage,* ed. John Haffenden, 291. London: Routledge & Kegan Paul, 1983.

Tagg, John. *The Burden of Representation: Essays on Photographies and Histories*. Amherst: Univ. of Massachusetts Press, 1988.

Tate, Alan, et al. "Sixteen Comments on Auden." *New Verse* 26–27 (1937): 23–30.

Thomas, Hugh. *The Spanish Civil War.* New York: Harper, 1961.

Thompson, E. P. "Outside the Whale." In *Out of Apathy,* ed. Norman Birnbaum, 141–94. London: Stevens, 1960.

———. *William Morris: Romantic to Revolutionary.* 1955. New York: Pantheon, 1977.

Tolley, A. T. *The Poetry of the Thirties*. New York: St. Martin's, 1975.

Trotter, David. *The Making of the Reader: Language and Subjectivity in Modern American, English and Irish Poetry*. Hong Kong: Macmillan, 1984.

Walkowitz, Judith R. *City of Dreadful Delight: Narratives of Sexual Danger in Late-Victorian London*. Chicago: Univ. of Chicago Press, 1992.

Warner, Rex. "Arms in Spain" and "The Tourist Looks at Spain." In *Poems for Spain,* ed. Stephen Spender and John Lehmann, 50, 65–69. London: Hogarth, 1939.

Waugh, Evelyn. "On a Pantomime Appearance, Mr. Isherwood and Friend." Review of *Journey to a War,* by W. H. Auden and Christopher Isherwood. In *W. H. Auden: The Critical Heritage,* ed. John Haffenden, 288–91. London: Routledge & Kegan Paul, 1983.

Waugh, Thomas. "Joris Ivens' *The Spanish Earth:* Committed Documentary and the Popular Front." In *"Show Us Life": Toward a History and Aesthetics of the Committed Documentary,* ed. Thomas Waugh, 105–32. Metuchen NJ: Scarecrow, 1984.

———. "Water, Blood, and War: Documentary Imagery of Spain from the North American Popular Front." In *The Spanish Civil War and the Visual Arts,* ed. Kathleen Vernon, 14–24. Western Societies Program Occasional Paper 24. Ithaca: Center for International Studies, Cornell University, 1990.

Weeks, Jeffrey. *Sex, Politics and Society: The Regulation of Sexuality since 1800*. 2d ed. London: Longman, 1989.

Whelan, Richard. *Robert Capa: A Biography*. New York: Knopf, 1986.

Willemen, Paul. "Presentation." In *British Cinema: Traditions of Independence,* ed. Don Macpherson and Paul Willemen, 1–5. London: British Film Institute, 1980.

Williamson, Judith. *Consuming Passions: The Dynamics of Popular Culture.* London: Boyars, 1985.

Winston, Brian. *Claiming the Real: The Griersonian Documentary and Its Legitimations.* London: British Film Institute, 1995.

Woods, Gregory. *Articulate Flesh: Male Homo-eroticism and Modern Poetry.* New Haven: Yale Univ. Press, 1987.

Woolf, Virginia. *Three Guineas.* 1938. Reprint, New York: Harcourt Brace, 1966.

Wright, George T. *W. H. Auden.* New York: Twayne, 1969.

Yates, Michael. "Iceland 1936." In *W. H. Auden: A Tribute,* ed. Stephen Spender, 59–68. New York: Macmillan, 1974.

Yeats, W. B. *Selected Poems and Two Plays of William Butler Yeats.* Ed. M. L. Rosenthal. New York: Collier, 1962.

INDEX